Journals
in the Classroom

Journals
in the Classroom

A Complete Guide
for the Elementary Teacher

Judith Ann Isaacs
Janine S. Brodine

PEGUIS
PUBLISHERS

Winnipeg   Manitoba   Canada

Printed and bound in Canada by Hignell Printing Limited on recycled paper. ✪

97 98   5   4   3   2

Canadian Cataloguing in Publication Data

Isaacs, Judith, 1941–

    Journals in the classroom

    Includes bibliographical references.
    ISBN 1-895411-69-6

1. Children – Diaries. 2. English language – Composition and exercises – Study and teaching (Elementary). 3. Language arts (Elementary). I. Brodine, Janine, 1950– II. Title.

LB1576.I72   1994   372.6'23   C94-920197-9

Book and Cover Design: Laura Ayers
Cover illustration: Me-map by Leahe Doran, Grade 3,
    Seattle Public Schools

Peguis Publishers Limited
100–318 McDermot Avenue
Winnipeg, Manitoba
Canada R3A 0A2

To John and Marc

Thanks for reading,
for commenting,
for enduring the process.

CONTENTS

W e are great believers in the use of journals in the classroom. Writing in journals encourages students to find their own voices, promotes writing fluency, and instills confidence. Too often, many would-be writers see writing as difficult and laborious—having to follow a set of rules for grammar, spelling, and punctuation. That response censors the writer and dampens the creative process; ideas are never put to paper. In journaling, students focus on the uninhibited expression of their thoughts and ideas.

Keeping a journal is the perfect way to establish a routine writing workout. Practicing writing is like shooting baskets—the more you do it, the better you get. Think of that ten-year-old who spends hours at the playground or in the driveway, hurling a basketball toward an impossibly high target. For weeks, years maybe, the ball seldom sinks through the hoop. But slowly, accuracy and skill improve. The young athlete learns new tricks, tries new shots from new locations. Every coach knows the only way to get to this point is to practice, practice, practice. Why should writing be different?

It is unrealistic to expect a student's writing to improve by scribbling for only a few minutes once a week. And it is outside the realm of possibility that writing will improve by completing work sheets that ask a child to underline the noun and verb or insert a comma correctly in a sentence. Teaching grammar is not the same as teaching writing. The way to become a better writer is to write, write, write.

As teachers in a large urban school district, we struggled to provide authentic writing experiences for our students. Then, in 1987, drawing on our own experience with keeping journals, we started teaching a course called The Power of

x

Personal Journals to adults in community colleges. We were also inspired to experiment in our journals and in our teaching after reading *The New Diary* by Tristine Rainier.

One day we recognized that we were living with a solution to the problem of providing regular writing practice to the young students in our public school classrooms. Of course! Make journal writing a regular part of the classroom regime but teach students a variety of journaling techniques. Give them a repertoire of writing strategies to keep journal writing fresh and interesting.

We first shared this idea with other teachers in 1989 when we designed a course for Seattle Pacific University. This course, Using Journals in the Classroom, is the genesis of this book.

We have talked with several hundred elementary teachers about their use of journals. They all believe that there is no better way to provide practice time for writers. These teachers are excited to see their students writing more—and liking it. Journals take the act of writing out of the language arts "box" and spread it throughout the day. Writing, like reading, becomes a part of every lesson.

Others reported they had "tried it once" and had become discouraged because the children didn't "take to it"; however, after further analysis, they realized that their goals had been overly ambitious. They found themselves better able to integrate journals into the daily routine after they developed guidelines and learned more about managing the process.

The main thrust of this book is to describe specific types of and techniques for journal writing. We also suggest guidelines for introducing and managing journals. Students go through huge developmental changes from kindergarten to grade six, and not every writing activity is appropriate for every age. We are confident that you can adapt these journaling ideas to fit your own classroom situation. We believe that all teachers can find a place for journals in their classrooms.

Our advice is to go slowly, introduce one idea at a time, and allow both the children and yourself to become comfortable with journaling. Keep thinking of how those basketballs bounce off the backboard and expect to see as many misses as scores. You're the coach. Set high expectations and be patient with the process. You will soon see your students gain fluency and confidence.

Many teachers throughout the Pacific Northwest have contributed to *Journals in the Classroom* with their inspiration and encouragement. Others have contributed samples of student work, guidelines, mission statements, and lessons or wisdom gleaned from their own work with journals. Still others read and commented on the text as it progressed. We thank all of you and all the students who have taken the Using Journals in the Classroom course.

✐ For contributing student samples: Roberta Colthurst, Marcene DuBois, Jerry Dunlap, Jan Gable, Marilyn Holms, Sharon Loen, Diane Miller, Carol Montante, Elane Murphy, Lyle Odegaard, June Simon, May Veazey, Mary Vestor, Janice Vetter, Joan Watson, Karen Wiley.

✐ For guidelines, mission statements, and quotes: Denise Abbey, Carolyn Burr, Roberta Colthurst, Marcene DuBois, Jan Gable, Mary Moore, Opal Oss, Sylvia Starr, Tammy Swant, Stacy Wood.

✐ For units and lessons: Cami Adkisson, Diane Baerwald, Joni Flory, Adrienne Gillet, Charlynne Hermann, Marie Hohnstein, Sharon Leithauser, Mary Moore, Leslie Osborne, Opal Oss, Sylvia Starr, Stacy Wood.

✐ For reading, editing, and drawing happy faces on our text: Nancy Crabtree, Pat Guild, and Sherrie Murray.

✐ And for showing us how one school puts it all together, a special thanks to the staff at Kimball School: teachers Peter Hubbard, Tina Merdinyan, Chris Morningstar, Jan Perry, and Leslie Rake; head teacher John Nakamura; and principal Victoria Foreman.

In Olaf Kendall's kindergarten class children sit around circular tables, heads bent to the task of writing in their journals. Each child has a standard piece of paper: the upper half blank, the lower half lined for printing.

Olaf circulates among his pupils and notes that Christa has drawn an enigmatic shape and is busily scrawling wavy lines below it. Across the table, Hieu has printed his name clearly at the top and is printing a string of capital letters, most of which sit on the top blue line. Olaf returns to his desk, opens his own journal, and adds a few lines to the draft of a poem he will share with the class later.

At the same time fourth-graders down the hall are writing in their journals too. Their task is more structured: they have been asked to write their feelings about the math lesson just completed. While they write, Jan Bennett, their teacher, and Maria Grand, her aide, are writing in their own journals, making notes on their observations of how each child has processed the day's lesson.

Each teacher chooses his or her own way of using journals in the classroom, and these journals take many different forms. In some classrooms they are like *personal diaries* in which students record their private thoughts. The journaling requirement is satisfied if the teacher sees the students writing daily. At the other end of the continuum are *highly structured learning logs*, in which students respond to specific questions provided by the teacher, who in turn reads and assesses the quality and quantity of their responses. In between these two extremes are journals used in the following ways:

🖉 *personal journals* in which students track their growth toward certain goals, which may or may not be shared with the teacher or class

🖉 *journals as responses to literature* in which students write their feelings and thoughts about a book they are reading

🖉 *journals used as writers' notebooks*, in which students practice techniques learned from other writers, making sketches, notes, and lists from which to draw material for first drafts

🖉 *dialogue journals* in which English as a second language (ESL) students gain language skills by exchanging written messages with their teachers

🖉 *team journals* in which students working in groups record the progress of their history projects, using one section to enter research findings, one section to brainstorm ideas, and one section to share feelings about how the group is doing

Journals are sometimes referred to as *logs*, but whether they are called journals or logs, their purpose is the same: to advance students' communication and thinking skills. Because language is the currency of our interactions in all of life's arenas, those who are deficient in reading, writing, listening, or speaking are greatly limited. The use of journals can greatly enhance all aspects of language study.

LEARNING TO WRITE

While teachers have always known that some children start school with the ability to read and write, they assumed that these children were precocious or the products of overachieving parents. Teacher training and popular wisdom have long promoted the belief that children should be taught to read according to a structured system adopted by a school district. Using a basal reader, children mastered basic skills and only then were allowed to choose books to read. In this time-honored approach, reading or reading preparation started in preschool or kindergarten. Once children achieved some competence in reading skills, the teacher's attention turned to writing instruction. Not until children had learned to form letters, write a few words, and understand the meaning of "sentence" were they free to compose their own writing.

Educators now realize that the writing readiness of many children doesn't fit this admittedly oversimplified plan of instruction. Children come to school eager to "write" all kinds of messages—signs, lists, stories, letters to friends. Using scribbles or whatever letters they can print, they happily produce their personal versions of writing and are excited to "read" their compositions. Observant teachers realize that many children arrive at school having already grasped the idea that when people make marks on paper, the marks have permanent meaning—something both the writer and others understand. Children's reading and writing readiness begins long before they pass through the schoolhouse door (Strickland 1990; Tompkins 1990).

> Think for a moment how writing is taught…first letters, then words, then sentences, then stories, then themes. On what information about writing development in children is this based? As far as I can determine, none. It is, instead, apparently the result of an attempt to think through from an adult logical viewpoint what would be reasonable for children to learn first. Unfortunately, in all too many cases, this prevents children from learning the *processes* into which they could feed increasingly complex pieces of data, whether they be linguistic forms, cognitive structure, or social and cultural information about the world. (Farr 1984)

Parents do not deny toddlers the opportunity to speak until after they have mastered the principles of grammar. By the same token, educators must not use children's lack of basic skills as a reason to restrain them from writing.

4

Our own observations support current thinking: children acquire reading and writing skills from their environment and the help of nurturing adults in much the same way they learn to listen and speak. They approximate adult speech ("Jana see Dadda on car"), they are reinforced, and corrected, with a response ("Yes, you see Daddy in the car"), and over time they gain more control of the conventions of the English language (Calkins 1986).

Many beginning readers can "read" books far beyond their tested grade level by using a combination of phonics, sight words, picture clues, and the memorization of familiar tales. In the same way, beginning writers, who don't know a sentence from an equation, draw on their limited repertoires: initial consonants, sight words, pictures, scribbles. Teachers who use journals accept that "...the novice is not totally unprepared to learn how to engage in reading and writing. Young readers have a rich knowledge of their world and a thorough tacit knowledge of speech and syntax." (Aulls 1985)

Journals provide the perfect vehicle for the tentative forays of fledgling writers. Here they can try out all those new discoveries, such as what happens when you put a space between words. Wow! It looks almost exactly like what the teacher wrote on the chalkboard. In the ongoing process of learning to write, the journal becomes the vessel in that voyage of discovery.

After children reach the intermediate grades and master the basics, the use of journals supports their exploration of more advanced writing skills. Researchers have studied children who acquired skills in mechanics and usage through regular, consistent writing practice, such as journaling or other original writing. When skill lessons evolved organically from their own personal writing, these children scored as high or higher on standardized tests as children who had been instructed using what many teachers think of as traditional methods (Calkins 1986; Sandmark and Coon 1988; Tompkins 1990). Journal writing is ideal for the practice and experimentation essential to natural writing development.

THE READING–WRITING CONNECTION

Learning to read is essential to success in school, and reading instruction, quite rightly, has received greater emphasis than any other subject. Many writers and researchers believe that writing enhances students' reading mastery in several ways (Tiedt et al 1989; Tierney et al 1989).

When they first try to communicate in writing, children begin by using the few sight words they know. They continually seek to learn more by reading whatever words they find in the environment, which in turn expands their writing vocabularies. At breakfast, Latisha, age four, reads "kids" from the cereal box. Keenan, age three, finds the word "video" in an advertisement on a bus. At the next opportunity these children have to write, they attempt to replicate these words. Beginning writers often use an initial letter sound to represent a word and then progress to the key consonants, essentially mimicking the process of reading phonetically. Children are accustomed to drawing pictures to communicate meaning, and they eventually discover that the pictures in books give clues to decoding the words. In these ways, learning to read and write becomes a reciprocal process.

Children who share their writing with others are motivated to improve both their reading and their writing skills. They want to be able to read the writing of their peers, and they ardently desire to have their writing read with comprehension. A routine of sharing journal entries sets in motion a reading-writing snowball that gains momentum as it continues through the year. Buddy journals, where students exchange journal entries, and dialogue journals, where a student and the teacher write to each other, are the ultimate forms of this kind of journaling. Classroom observation has shown that children are able to read and respond appropriately to teachers' replies even if those replies are written at a higher reading level than their basal readers (Staton 1987).

As children learn to read like writers, they become better writers themselves. In their journals, students may write about the books they read and those read to them. Intermediate students may try their hands at writing in the style of a favorite author or may imitate a new genre presented in the classroom. As students analyze others' writing with the thought of using the results of such analysis in their own writing, their comprehension and sophistication deepen. For this reason many teachers now use literature as a springboard for writing as well as a substitute for basal readers.

Several children in John Cook's second-grade class notice funny marks at the beginning and end of some sentences in one of their favorite books. This provides an opening for him to teach a mini-lesson on using quotation marks. During the next few journaling sessions, quotation marks sprout like weeds. After hearing a mystery read by their teacher in a fifth-grade classroom, those children who are more practiced writers try to create suspenseful stories in their next journal entries.

After a class reads a book or story together, the teacher can direct students' thinking by asking leading questions: Is the meaning clear? What is the writer's intent? What else do you want to know? The students then think about and discuss how the author crafted meaning. Children can, if taught to do so, use similar skills to discuss their own writing. In sharing journal entries, whether with an individual or a small group, they can ask the same kinds of questions: What do you mean in this part? How did you want us to feel? Would you put in more about...? By encouraging these questions in both readers' and writers' conferences, you will strengthen the transference of learning between reading and writing (Blackburn 1984; Tierney 1990).

LEARNING TO THINK

Language and thinking are inextricably entwined. In schools students are usually asked to demonstrate their mastery of knowledge and the results of their thinking through speaking or writing.

> The more people write the better they learn. Of all the modes of language use, writing is the most powerful for developing sustained critical thought. It is writing that makes our thought visible and helps us to modify, extend, develop, or critique that thought. (Fulwiler 1986)

Thinking skills have received a lot of attention in recent years. Noting that our children lack critical thinking skills, we have undertaken to teach them how to think. Many educators also recognize that the drill sheets used in many content areas teach only the lower-level thinking skills of recall and recognition. The result has been an onslaught of activities and exercises designed to encourage higher-level thinking skills.

In journals students have the opportunity to practice the whole range of thinking skills. More than one writing teacher has said that good writing is good thinking (Fulwiler 1986; Moffett 1992). Certain skills have been identified as higher-order processes: synthesis, speculation, evaluation, classifying, invention, hypothesizing (Bloom 1977; Raths, Wasserman, Arthur, and Rothstein 1986). Good writing requires the use of all those skills.

> We should *enable* youngsters to abstract at as high a level as they are capable of so that they have maximum range and choice, but this goal does not at all imply that they should abandon kinds of writing they learned earlier…Every authentic writing activity can be done at many levels of maturity. (Moffett 1992)

What kinds of journaling foster higher-level thinking? Teachers in kindergarten through grade six have many options. The following are only a few of the ways in which critical thinking skills can be developed in journals:

🖉 In a fourth-grade classroom children use journals to *explain* a division equation in words.

🖉 A fifth-grade teacher asks students to take out their journals and spend five minutes at the end of the social studies period to *summarize* in their own words what they learned that day.

🖉 Second-graders use a page in their journals to *classify* words from their own previous journal entries according to similar initial sounds.

🖉 ESL students use their journals to *examine their assumptions* about North American culture and language.

🖉 Sixth-graders *imagine* themselves in another person's place to try to understand what it was like to be an African American living in Memphis in the 1960s.

🖉 Third-graders write in buddy journals in a shared process to *evaluate* the consequences of certain playground behaviors.

Journals also are good places for the practice of meta-cognition, in which we examine and reflect on our own thinking and learning processes. Students use them to explain how to solve problems of all kinds. For example, fourth-graders record how they decided which operation to use in a story problem taken from their math text. The next day the same students write to buddies about ways to get along better with bossy older siblings.

Jan Gable, a first-grade teacher, wrote in her journal that

> thinking is a multi-phased process and for many of us thinking can be extended or clarified with pencil in hand. Writing can give us an awareness of our own thoughts and can allow us to hold these thoughts long enough to scrutinize them—in short to think about our own thinking...Thus we find that the tool (a journal) can begin to assist us in shaping our thoughts and possibly even our own behavior. This is a very powerful potential.

In chapter 5 we use a familiar model, Bloom's Taxonomy, and offer specific ideas for using journals in a variety of subjects with special attention to the inclusion of all levels of thinking.

COGNITIVE STYLES

In this book you will find an array of journal types and techniques. As with everything you present in the classroom, some students will take to one technique or type, others to a different one. In the act of choosing one over another, students are exhibiting variations in their cognitive preferences. One of the best reasons to teach a variety of journal entry types and techniques is to provide each child with a bag of tricks. This enables students to use whatever fits best with their preferred ways of learning.

Numerous researchers have described cognitive processes in terms of learning styles: holistic, analytic, personal, active, or hands-on. Holistic learners like the big picture; they work from whole to part. Analytic learners are just the opposite; they easily master detail and work from part to whole. Personal learners need to make a connection between their learning and their lives; relationships are in the forefront of their thinking. Active learners process information kinesthetically; it is important to give them opportunities to move. Hands-on learners like to get involved and experience things for themselves in a concrete way and to study real situations (Barbe and Swassing 1979; Butler 1988; Guild and Garger 1988).

Using a variety of journaling techniques is one way to accommodate the diverse learning-style needs found in every classroom. Personal learners often write about relationships and can't wait to share their entries; analytic learners like using logs to record data; hands-on learners prefer to be involved in an experience and to make on-site observations before turning to their journals; holistic learners, who naturally make associations between concepts, find the journal an ideal place to explore those linkages. Active learners may find it difficult to write and are more likely to be motivated by journaling about physical activities, such as sports.

When you provide a variety of journaling experiences, students have opportunities to use their individual strengths. When they are presented with only one way of learning a task or approaching a problem, some cognitive styles are inevitably neglected. For example, the strongest mode for holistic learners is to proceed from whole to part. Therefore, they will want to see how journal writing can be used in a variety of ways before moving to instruction in specific techniques.

Another approach to the way people learn comes from Howard Gardner (1983), who was the first to describe individual learner's strengths in terms of multiple intelligences. He postulates, persuasively, that each of us excels in one or more of seven intelligences: kinesthetic, logical/mathematical, verbal/linguistic, musical, spatial, interpersonal, intrapersonal. While some of the intelligences he identifies overlap with learning styles (interpersonal and personal learner, for example), his findings add a new dimension to learning theory.

The multiple intelligences concept is an excellent rationale for using journals in *every* subject—physical education, music, math, science—and for many purposes— exposition, reflection, problem solving, creative design. Journals allow those who are gifted in different ways to give voice to their strengths. Clearly, those whose strength is linguistic intelligence will be voluminous writers. Those with exceptional musical intelligence will have a special sensitivity to the nuances of music, which they can express in writing. Those with a strong spatial intelligence will be able to depict many of their thoughts graphically in their journals through drawing and diagramming. Others with a highly developed kinesthetic intelligence will have the rare ability to observe and interpret movement in dance or sports, activities that provide a natural introduction to the act of writing. Those with a high level of intrapersonal intelligence will be more likely to use their journals for reflection and introspection than will persons with intelligences highly developed in other areas.

SOCIAL DEVELOPMENT

The development of social skills, once somewhat of a hidden curriculum in schools, is becoming more and more overt as increasing numbers of children come to school lacking interpersonal skills. Educators are aware that children with high self-esteem learn better, and journals can play a role in helping students develop social skills and self-esteem. This is why many adults use personal journals to explore problems and their solutions or simply to release pent-up emotions. Children have the same needs and can use the same route. Some of the skills that can be developed through journals are sharing and following directions (for primary children) and negotiation, anger management, and resolving problems with friends (for intermediate children).

Through structured prompts and modeling, teachers can encourage students to use their journals to explore alternative solutions to conflict situations. For example, Lindsey Chao's sixth-grade class is in an uproar because name calling escalated into a fight between two classmates. The combatants are presently in the principal's office, but the class cannot settle down. Lindsey asks them to brainstorm with her a list of alternative courses of action that might have resulted in a different outcome. With that list before the class, she asks the students to write in their journals a scenario using one of the solutions and then share their ideas with those at their tables.

Using a "what-if" prompt allows children to rehearse problem-solving or decision-making skills in writing. They can ponder the consequences of their actions by writing answers to questions such as the following: What if I copy someone's book report? What if I cut ahead in line? What if someone makes me hand over my lunch money?

Just the act of journal writing is a boost to some youngsters' self-esteem. Children realize that class time is valuable, and the fact that class time is devoted to writing about *their* ideas is significant. Their thoughts are considered important enough to record! If they are in a classroom where they have an opportunity to dialogue with their teacher in a journal, the boost is even stronger. When their teacher writes back, they learn that someone really cares about what they think.

STUDENT-CENTERED LEARNING

The applications of journals we have discussed can change the climate of a classroom by making it more student-centered. Having had time to reflect in their journals, students ask more questions of their own and generate more ideas to guide the direction of their learning.

> When instructors give over class time to a discussion of ideas generated in non-graded journal writing, they are in fact altering the teacher-student relationship in important ways: student ideas command center stage along with instructor ideas and both are seen as legitimate and vital. (Fulwiler 1986)

Some teachers say their main goal in using journals is to give students time to reflect. In the crowded curriculum that exists in most schools, with allotted amounts of material to "cover," students and teachers feel continually rushed. Journal writing creates the quiet time so necessary for musing on the self. What's important to me? What do I need to know more about? How do I feel about myself and my school at this moment? Even very young students understand that in their journals they are being asked to be original, to share ideas that are uniquely their own.

CONCLUDING THOUGHTS

Teachers who consistently use journals find that the benefits are many. By reading even an occasional journal entry, they come to know their students better. When they ask students to write their feelings about the day or to explain a lesson, teachers get immediate feedback on how well the class has understood the teaching. Teachers can read questions and comments written by shy students who never find the courage to raise their hands and speak out in front of the whole class.

Our work with both students and teachers has confirmed Geddes's conclusion that using journals benefits children in the following ways:

1. Journals offer a powerful way to assess student knowledge at the higher levels of learning.

2. Journals effectively focus student attention on values, attitudes and ethical issues.

3. Journals provide for self-exploration and self-discovery.

4. Journals encourage students to think and require an articulation of their thoughts.

5. Journals make education personal.

6. Journals improve writing. (Geddes 1992)

Journals cannot do everything—no single teaching strategy is the panacea that solves all problems. But they can do a lot. In the chapters that follow we describe various ways of writing in journals—free writing, listing, webbing, altered point of view, unsent letters, close observation, and me-maps. These seven writing techniques can be used in four types of journals—individual journals, dialogue journals, buddy or team journals, and learning logs.

Think of this book as a road map for your venture into what may be for you unexplored territory. In the following pages you will find practical tips for introducing journals to your classroom, choosing topics, and developing a mission statement, as well as more than one hundred specific ideas for using journals in different content areas. We answer the questions we are asked most frequently and provide some ideas for integrating journals into a whole-language classroom and as part of your informal assessment process.

Most teachers are familiar with the type of journals in which students write for a specified amount of time in notebooks that are kept in their desks. These are known as individual journals. However, the introduction of other kinds of journals will expand their applications. The following are definitions of four key types of journals:

- *individual journal.* Students write each day on whatever they wish or whatever comes to mind in response to a prompt or topic suggested by the teacher.

- *dialogue journal.* Students write in much the same way as in an individual journal, although the statements and questions more often relate to school work. The teacher responds on a regular basis (daily or weekly) by writing in each student's journal.

- *learning log.* Students write ideas and questions that arise from classroom lessons, research, or assigned reading, frequently relating their personal experiences to learning. A learning log may take the form of a double-entry journal or may be written in paragraphs. The teacher may or may not choose to respond by writing in the learning log.

- *team or buddy journal.* A pair or group of students write in the same journal on a specific topic, engaging in written dialogue among themselves. The teacher may or may not choose to respond by writing in the journal.

INDIVIDUAL JOURNALS

The individual journal is truly that— personal; a confidant and friend through which students explore questions, fears, new ideas, and any other thoughts that race through their heads, whether or not these are related to school. These journals are shared only with the teacher. Typically, students write for ten or fifteen minutes a day in their journals. Periodically, the teacher collects the journals to review students' writing and make some kind of evaluation of the journals to factor into students' progress reports.

Some teachers assign topics to explore; others have students refer to a topic list or respond to a prompt on the board. Usually, students are given the choice of writing whatever they wish or using the prompt as a springboard. Their journal entries may involve any of the techniques described in chapter 3.

In the following example a third-grader wrote about an important happening in her life:

1-3-90

I lost my tooth on Chistmas vaicion. And I pulled it out my self. Then I put it under my pellow and I woke up next morning and I had a doller. Now I'v lost seven teeth. And I have anther tooth loues. Pretty soon I'll hare lost eight teeth. And that was the therd tooth. I pulled out my self my mom & dad are very proud of me and I'v saved all the money I got from the tooth fairey so I have seven dollar

Many younger writers illustrate their journal entries.
In the following examples lively drawings accompany
the text.

Rodorick   May 21-1991

in May   my   daddy
came   Home   and
I   was   happy   and He came
   in   a   Plaen

I lile ships and boas and pierit.
ships   it   is   fun   to   play   with
them   and   thay   can   flaot   in   the

May 23-

In the example, below,
another third-grader responded to a
prompt from his teacher who had
asked him about what he liked
about school. ("Receiveds" was a
creative spelling of "recesses.")

9-3-93 Joseph
School is
I like school   because   you   ge
to have   three   recelveds.

If journals are of the "Dear Diary" variety, students may be reluctant to share them with the teacher. One way to handle sensitive issues is to allow students to fold over the page if they wish their thoughts to remain confidential. You are then honor-bound to pass over that entry.

Teachers also give students an opportunity to ruminate on class work in their journals—to record their frustrations or joys. Individual journals can be integrated into all subject areas. Provide a prompt following a lesson such as "Tell me how you felt about the girl in the story we read today" or "How would you explain fractions to another student?"

If you are just beginning to use journals, start with individual journals. They are the easiest type to implement.

DIALOGUE JOURNALS

Many teachers have found dialogue journals to be a great way to motivate students to write (Bode 1989; Staton 1987). Students use dialogue journals in much the same way as individual journals. However, in dialogue journals the teacher writes a brief response in each journal. Soon dialogues—exchanges—are established, and student and teacher carry on conversations in writing. Most often the statements and questions relate to school work, although students sometimes seize the opportunity to share intimate thoughts and seek personal information from their teachers.

Dialogue journals also help students improve their reading skills. Even poor writers/readers are motivated by the opportunity to engage in a one-to-one dialogue with their teachers. By modeling correct spelling and form in your responses, you give students an opportunity to see appropriate usage, as in the example, left. Students often correct themselves in future entries.

> I like helppl Eugen it fun I like him he is nice, I wich I could do it agen next week. hoope he will get well soon.
>
> Dear Josh,
> You are really doing a great job by helping Eugene. I am sure he is happy to have you be his helper. It must be very hard for him to get around using crutches. I hope he will get well soon too.
>
> Mrs. Prochorow

Through dialogue journals teachers gain greater knowledge of their students. Quiet students who always stay on the periphery of things reveal themselves; introverted students take the opportunity to write questions. Many teachers say that they have come to know their students much better since they began using dialogue journals.

The dialogue journal answers the need of some learners to have a close relationship with their teacher. It also suits students who prefer to process new information by asking questions and making personal connections to their learning.

The downside of the dialogue journal is the paper-load problem. Twenty-five to forty students in each elementary classroom create a daunting pile of paper. Clearly, a good management system is needed. Most teachers love the idea of the dialogue journal, but are reluctant to make the commitment of time required to write even a few sentences to each of a large number of students. The following are some solutions to this problem:

- Collect journals from a portion of the class daily so that you then read only four to six journals each day.

- Write responses during journal-writing time instead of after school. Sit beside a student and write your entry on the spot.

- Ask volunteers (parents and older students) to respond to journal entries.

- Each week ask students to highlight or star one entry to which they would like you to respond.

BUDDY AND TEAM JOURNALS

In a buddy journal the dialogue takes place between two students instead of between a student and a teacher. Buddy journals take the onus off the teacher to be the sole responder to a large number of students. They give students the opportunity to get even more immediate feedback than dialogue journals provide and also motivate them by the opportunity to read their partners' entries. As with dialogue journals, students are involved in real writing done for the purpose of direct communication.

Here are the goals a sixth-grade teacher set for buddy journals:

- Build on students' natural abilities to converse orally.

- Provide a real audience and give students reasons to write legibly and coherently.

- Improve students' grammar, spelling, and punctuation.

- Promote student interaction, cooperation, and collaboration.

- Build interest and confidence.

- Allow students opportunities to share problems and insights as they begin to support and help each other.

Teachers have told us of the many changes they observe when these objectives are accomplished. Here is the comment made by teacher Roberta Colthurst:

> Each day four or five students would ask, "When are we going to do our journal writing?" Students who normally balk at any type of writing assignment and dawdle the entire time began reading and writing the moment they retrieved their journals...Most students became more conscious of their spelling since other students were going to read their entries. They often looked back in their journals to see how their buddies spelled a word or asked their neighbors to help them.

Another teacher, Carolyn Burr, wrote:

> The students cheer when I say it is buddy journal time. I have noticed one very slow student begin to form complete sentences in his journal writing. I have also seen students writing to each other about how to spell unfamiliar words.

Here's how it works. Two students who are journal buddies sit together, and each writes to the other for a specified time (usually only five minutes to start). Without speaking, they trade journals and write a response, stopping after another five minutes. Usually two rounds is sufficient for a meaningful exchange of ideas.

Ideally, when students are writing in their buddy journals, they do not communicate orally. However, in a class of students of varying skill levels, or with very young students, having the option of reading an entry to a buddy is a good idea.

Buddy journals call for careful preparation and clear rules, for example, no put-downs. We suggest that, at the beginning, teachers monitor exchanges to intercept any in which students are name-calling or denigrating their buddies. A conference with the offender followed by continued monitoring makes it clear that you expect the guidelines to be followed.

Teachers who use buddy journals retain the prerogative of assigning buddies and have found it best to change partners every two or three weeks. Those whose writing ability is limited or whose handwriting is poor may be left out otherwise. Some teachers hand out color-coded journals and ask students to find a buddy who has a journal the same color as theirs. Others simply draw names out of a hat or ask the class to number off. A variation is to ask all students to group themselves by birth month and then pick a buddy from within that group.

In the example at right, two students have a good exchange in their buddy journal, despite their differing ability levels. They are responding to a list of questions suggested by their teacher.

Get students off to a good start by suggesting topics (favorite food, game, and so on) or brainstorming a list of questions to write for a buddy to answer. Once students gain experience, they will generate their own topics, as in the example, left.

Most teachers use buddy journals for two or three weeks, alternating with individual and dialogue journals.

Team journals are usually assigned as part of a group project or activity. Each member of a four- or five-person team is responsible for writing his or her views about the project or new learning and to respond to other members of the team. The journals are kept in a central place where they are easily accessible.

> May 13, 199
>
> Dear buddy,
> I can't go to the
> Indian pot lactth
> But I can on thursday
> I love math do you?
> my favorite color
> is red and blue.
> what is your
> favorite Animal?
> your buddy,
> Danielle

LEARNING LOGS

All the types of journals described so far can be purely personal in content or a response to lessons. The learning log, however, is specifically about lessons: students respond to demonstrations, videos, or, most often, reading assignments.

In this type of journal, students have an opportunity to go beyond answering the questions at the end of the chapter. For example, Kathleen Beck's fifth-graders use their learning logs as they read about Brazil in their social studies textbooks. She wants them to think about the reading rather than to "take notes." Mohammed likes this type of journal and is quick to get started. After drawing a line vertically down the center of a page of his journal, he enters interesting words or phrases from the text in the left column as he reads. In the right column he makes brief notes of his reactions to the ideas and words, questions, comparisons, and whatever else comes to mind. Here are some of his entries:

> *I don't think they should cut the rain forest, because the earth needs it.*

> *Their Indians lose homes just like here in the Old West days.*

> *How long would it take to go up the Amazon? I'd be amazed to see a pink dolphin!*

This type of learning log is sometimes called a double-entry journal.

Very often, children use learning logs to record their responses to stories they read or hear. In the example, left, a second-grader who had read about Frankenstein, wrote a question that occurred to him in the left column, and answered it on the right.

24

Many teachers ask students to write a paragraph in their journals in response to a lesson or a story. In some classrooms this is called a learning log, albeit a less structured form. In another social studies lesson, for example, a student wrote the following in response to a video about Samoa:

> Being Samoan: Video
>
> Samoan people are almost just like us. Samoan peop are prod for who thay are. And Samoa has stors and its almos just like USa. But thay do do alot of things that there andsisters did. Samoa has changed since there andsiters time. The andsisters the things thay need where shelter, close, food. But now thay need money in the time of the andsisters thay did't have money thay traded.

When teachers write responses in these journals, the learning logs take on some of the characteristics of dialogue journals. In the example below a student wrote about a book the teacher read, and the teacher responded to the journal entry.

> Javon
>
> Abiyoyo
> The boy and his father went to Abiyoyo then the boy ran to Abiyoyo Abiyoyo tird to get the boy but he missed and fell dwon then the father took his wand out and Zoop his head disapeird then Zoop his arm was gone, then Zoop! his other arm was gone Zoop his legs were gone Zoop his body was gone.
>
> Wow! Jaron, I like the the way you had Abiyoyo disappear. Who did Abiyoyo try to get before he fell down?

The use of learning logs avoids rote learning by forcing students to form an opinion or to articulate a personal response to a classroom presentation. Students are guided to higher-level thinking skills by being asked to reflect, for example, on how a science lesson about the ecology of the rain forest relates to a novel in that setting. At another time, they may compare and contrast a current assignment to a previous reading or speculate on alternative outcomes. Logs also provide structure and promote participation during small-group discussions and other cooperative learning activities. When students are asked to read from their learning logs, everyone has something to say.

As with all types of journals, start by modeling the kind of entries you expect. It is helpful to present a log containing responses from the whole class using an overhead projector or the chalkboard so all students can see the process.

The following guidelines for learning logs were prepared by Sylvia Starr, a third-grade teacher:

> On the chalkboard I write student-generated responses reviewing what was done and what happened during a lesson. Using spiral notebooks, students draw a line down the middle of a page. On the left side of the page, the students copy the review from the board. On the right side, students write their comments, opinions, questions, or previous experiences they have had relating to that particular phase of the lesson.

> Learning logs are of a factual nature and do not require confidentiality. In fact, the students often share them in small groups or with the whole class.

> The primary purpose of learning logs is for the students to reflect on the previous lesson as well as create a record they can refer to for later assignments. Therefore, these journals are not graded. I write a weekly response in each child's journal.

CONCLUDING THOUGHTS

Individual journals remain the most flexible of the four journal types discussed in this chapter because they are easiest to manage. While many teachers use only this model, other teachers introduce a specific type of journal for a particular purpose. For example, buddy journals can be used to support a theme of honoring differences, while dialogue journals might be introduced at the beginning of the year to get to know students. Many teachers use learning logs as a way for students to respond to literature. Choose the type of journal to use on the basis of the grade level you teach and the learning objective you are addressing. Because different students respond to different types of journals, be sure to give each a try.

The journals are ready. Blank pages await young writers, some of whom are eager, others reluctant. We recommend seven writing techniques for use in journals. Some, possibly all, will be familiar to you. They are not newly invented writing strategies but ones we have found to be especially suited to journaling:

- *free writing:* a free flow of ideas in prose form

- *listing:* lists of ideas or images on a given topic

- *webbing:* words or phrases centered around a central topic and recorded randomly

- *altered point of view:* prose written from the perspective of an inanimate object or real or imagined being

- *unsent letters:* letters composed of thoughts, ideas, and feelings written to a real or imaginary person

- *close observation:* description that incorporates many sensory details

- *me-maps:* non-verbal drawings using pictures or symbols to represent feelings or observations

Some students will be motivated to work with all these techniques, but don't be surprised if, for example, one loves "close observation" and hates "unsent letters." Another's pencil may fly at every opportunity for "free writing" but drop in dismay at the prospect of drawing a "me-map" that requires the expression of ideas without words. Introduce the seven techniques over the course of a few months. Once students have a repertoire of journal techniques, they will be able to choose those that are their best and favorite vehicles of expression.

FREE WRITING

For those who use journals in either their personal lives or the classroom, free writing is perhaps the most familiar of the techniques described in this chapter. Free writing is simply the process of committing to paper a flow of words while quieting the internal critic who insists on correct spelling, punctuation, and grammar. Students write without lifting pen from paper. The goal is to capture fleeting thoughts without editing or analyzing. Invented spellings are allowed, as are creative uses of punctuation and grammar. Phrases or single words—separated by commas, dots, or spaces—are fine. The flow mimics the thought process. Content is more important than conventions of standard written English.

For many journal writers, feeling successful in free writing takes time; it is a process. Once students see the lines of their journals fill with words, their confidence increases, as does the fluidity of their writing.

In the following example, a fifth-grader tries to keep up with her thoughts:

> *I am not sure what to write. This is not as easy as it sounds. I am reading a good book now. I would much rather read that book than write this. The book is almost like calling me. "Christy, read me!" I want to, too. What should I write about now? Some things I can't write because they are too personal. My thoughts are going by faster than I can catch them. This is kind of weird. I don't understand why you want us to write this. I have to tell you that this will not help you understand me better. Michelle gave me the idea to write about food and now I can't get it off my mind. "The wheel is gonna get ya, the wheel is gonna get you tonight!" Gummy bears, hopping here and there and everywhere. Sorry about that but that just came to mind.*

One of your roles is to encourage output rather than accuracy. Forget editing for now. At a later date free writing can be lifted from the journal for further development if you wish. The section titled "The Writing Process" in chapter 8 offers specific suggestions on how to do this.

If you or some of your students are uncomfortable with totally free writing, give students a choice of having the reader, whether it is you or a classmate, correct errors. You might want to duplicate a short checklist like the following:

☐ No corrections, please.

☐ Correct spelling errors.

☐ Correct grammatical errors.

Students then attach the checklists either to the inside covers of their journals or to a specific entry. Thus, readers can respond to each student's specific request or need for feedback on mechanics.

At left is a free-writing example written by a first-grader.

Below is another example by an older child.

Amelia And I May 21,1990
One morning when at morning resess Amelia and I went on the rings and monkey bars. Then Amelia spent the night we drew houses and dogs and horses. The next day we went on the rings and monkey bars agin and agin. THE
N
D

good bye!

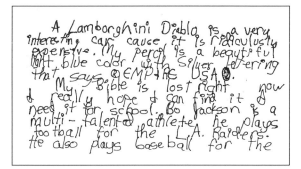

A Lamborghini Diablo is a very interesting car cause it is ridiculusly expensive. My perol is a beautiful light blue color with silver lettering that says EMPIRE USA. My Bible is lost right now I really hope I can find it I need it for school. Bo Jackson is a multi-talented athlete he plays football for the L.A. Raiders. He also plays baseball for the

Some students take to free writing quickly, while others may need prompts. If students say they don't know what to write, ask them to start with that sentence, writing it again and again if necessary. The response may well look like this: "I don't know what to write. Oh, I've got an idea. Well, today this one man started pointing his finger at me." Another option is to suggest writing about how they "feel right now." Offer some suggestions to help them get going (warm, happy, cold, quiet, tired).

Students need lots of practice with free writing to become comfortable with it. This technique is important as it is used in other kinds of journaling, including altered point of view and unsent letters.

Free writing has two principal forms: unfocused and focused. In unfocused free writing, content ebbs and flows without following a single course. Any thought is relevant. Often, the writing will end on a very different topic than it began.

The purpose of focused free writing is to explore all options on a given subject. This is different from unfocused free writing because writers are expected to stay on a single topic, whether assigned by the teacher or chosen by the student.

Topics are endless and range from "My House" or "Recess" to "A Time I Needed Courage," depending on the grade level. For example, when first-graders were directed to tell about their favorite animals and about similarities between the animals and themselves using a minimum of two sentences and a picture, the following were two of their responses: "My favorite best is the tiger. We both have ears" and "My favorite beast is the leopard. We both have teeth."

Varying your prompts helps everyone get started. Some students first give voice to their thoughts and then make a transition to the written word. "Tell me about something you might want to write about" followed by a minute or two of listening may be all the encouragement they need.

For students who prefer visual stimuli, have a file of magazine pictures available. Others may respond to "Draw me a picture of something you want to write about" and be inspired by doodling for a while before putting words to paper.

Another popular way to introduce focused free writing is to read a story together and then ask students to write about what happened. Their journals become arenas for

reliving their favorite story experiences or getting reacquaint-
ed with favorite characters.

Free writing can become an avenue for experimenting
with form. On Tuesday a third-grader chose to write in
verse:

> *I like to write poems. here's one:*
> *There was an old man*
> *who lived in a shoe, he*
> *liked to ride horses and*
> *I do too!*

Later that week the same third-grader wrote in narrative
form:

> *When I was in the first grade I was trying to do the*
> *cherry drop with someone holding on to my hands and*
> *they let go and I feel and nocked the wind out of me and*
> *I went home and the next day I went to school and I had*
> *bad pains for a long time.*

An exciting way to encourage older students' fluency and
amount of writing is to set a time limit for free writing.
When you first introduce the technique, set a timer for at
least ten minutes. Students are generally surprised to see
how much they can get on paper in that amount of time.
Some students seem to thrive on the challenge and implied
competition; others like the structure of a time limit.
Whether you incorporate journals in your classroom once a
week or every day, increase the time in one- or two-minute
increments until sessions last up to thirty minutes.

Modeling promotes students' journal writing. If at all
feasible, make entries in your own journal while your
students are writing. If you aren't able to write with them
during every journaling session, try to participate during
at least the first few sessions. In any case, be prepared to
share some of your entries when you introduce free writing
and occasionally throughout the year. Showing that
journaling is important to you increases the likelihood that
it will become important to your students.

LISTING

In journal writing, listing serves a dual function: a way to brainstorm various topics and a journaling technique in and of itself. Whether compiling lists individually or in groups, students generate many ideas quickly. Another advantage of listing is that it frees less skilled students from the constraints of sentence structure, grammar, and standard English.

Personal interest prompts are a good way to begin. A third-grader created this list of topics using the prompt "I like to write about...":

1. Clifford
2. school
3. poems
4. unicorns
5. rainbows
6. waterfalls
7. castles
8. queens, princesses, kings, and princes
9. parties
10. bodys
11. Mrs. Loen
12. me and my family
13. how to write—supercalafradgalisticexpealdoshes

The following list was produced by a sixth-grader:

1. People I love
2. The day I forgot my homework
3. When I had an accident
4. My worst injury
5. Friends
6. Vacation
7. What's in the alley?
8. Pets I had
9. Why is sixth grade so much fun for sixth-graders?
10. Bad dreams
11. What's a best friend and what's a good friend?
12. Kinds of clothes

13. *Ways I put up my hair*
14. *Foods I like*
15. *Foods I don't like*

Personal topic lists such as these can be attached to the inside cover of each journal, allowing easy access to topic ideas. Having students generate their own topics develops immediate "ownership" and also builds self-esteem by showing students that their topics are as valid as the teacher's. In chapter 4, page 56, you'll find a "list of lists" and a detailed explanation of how to generate topics.

Some teachers report that listing is an easier way to introduce journaling than free writing. Listing ideas instead of creating sentences can be less intimidating for reluctant writers. Gazing at a blank page creates a block in writers of any age, whether they are writing informally in a journal or preparing an essay. Primary students who are building vocabularies but lack confidence about their sentence structure are able to create lengthy lists. For example, a second-grader came up with the list below.

The process for introducing listing is very similar to that for free writing. Students are to write any thoughts that come to mind. The ideas are paramount; creative spelling and grammar are fine.

An extension is to guide students through a double-list process.

```
10-18-96  I  like  Halloween  because
1. I get candy
2. It is scairare.
3. Pumpkns
4. It is fun.
5. Scattas.
6. Gosts
7. It is sceaire
8. Vapiers
9. Some time Someone can jump
10. thair are scaire books.
11. pirits
12.
```

Using a self-chosen or teacher-assigned topic, have students take five to ten minutes to write a list. Invite your journal writers to share their lists with the class or buddies. (This is particularly interesting when they have started with the same topic.) Then ask students to choose one of their newly listed ideas as the impetus for a second list. This will help students understand how to narrow the focus, a skill they will use later in writing compositions.

Here's one way it can work. A fourth-grade class has just completed a unit on astronomy. They first list all the planets they can think of. On the second list students shift from the scientific to the literary by picking a planet from their list and listing adjectives that describe it. Another option would be for students to write about the kinds of beings that might inhabit the planet if it had life on it. A related option would be to ask students to write about traveling from Earth to the planet.

Listing often appeals to children who prefer to learn about parts before they get to a whole, to those who are more comfortable when their ideas are lined up rather than sprawled across a page.

WEBBING

Webbing is a non-linear technique also known as mind mapping or clustering. While free writing records ideas in prose form and listing records them in a linear mode, webbing allows the writer to explore and note random thoughts in a more graphic fashion. Writers develop and expand concepts; they create new relationships among ideas. Webs can be journal entries in and of themselves; they may also be springboards for free writing.

The process requires an 8 1/2-by-11 inch (22 cm-by-28 cm) blank sheet of paper, or larger, and pen, pencil, or colored markers. Writers place a topic phrase or key word in the center of the paper and circle it. They then respond to the central word by recording the first image, feeling, or expression that comes to mind.

In the example shown below the central idea was summer. A student created this web by writing four subheadings: *Vacation, Hot, Fun,* and *Beach.* She then concentrated on each subheading, writing all the ideas that came to mind as fast as she could. For example, vacation made her think of *Orcas Island,* which then led to *camp, summer cabin,* and *beautiful.*

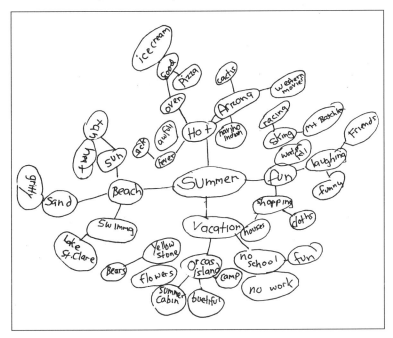

By definition, webs are done randomly; their final forms will be as diverse as the people who design them. The webs, next page, both began with the word *space.* In the first web, the student recorded the ideas that came to him when he thought of space: *hangers, desk, dresser,* and *closet,* which led to *room.* If we follow his web in a counterclockwise direction, we are led to the circled ideas: *atoms, aliens, studies, spaceship, travel,* and *outer space.* Interspersed among these concepts are explanations about aliens, planets, and astronomy. In the second example the student drew a heart around *space.* He then drew various kinds of linkages to his ideas. A string of small hearts leads to *field, moon, stars,* and *sun.* In the upper left, diamonds and oblongs stretch to reach *forest, states, bookbag,* and *box.* In a random fashion, he recorded a range of images from *zoo* to *balloons.* Each

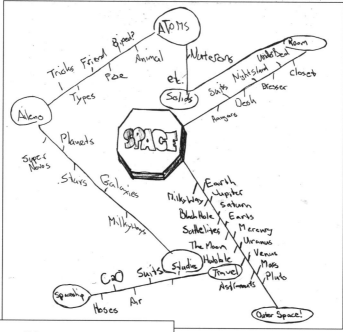

relates to the concept of space, either directly or indirectly.

In other webs students may think of a flow of ideas that relate to one another, and words may cascade to a corner of the page. Only one or two ideas may appear in the upper half of the web. No matter what the final appearance, the process is the same: ideas, images, and feelings are recorded as they occur; the internal critic is silenced until the web is complete.

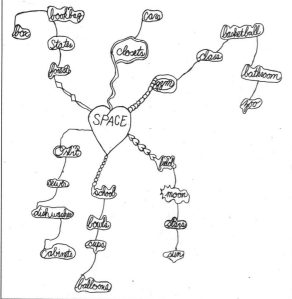

A webbing variation similar to double listing is to have students choose one area of their webs to expand. The student who drew the last example might choose the word *zoo*. He would then begin a new web with *zoo* as the central focus.

To introduce webbing, first lead a class in a group assignment. The secret to success in this strategy is to choose a common experience as a stimulus. If a group of students has read a book together, gone on a recent field trip, or listened to a speaker, choose that as the central topic.

Don't let students give up too quickly. Ask them to keep adding to their webs for a minimum amount of time, at least five minutes. Sometimes they will discover that their best ideas are those on the fringes of the web.

This is how Stacy Wood, a fourth-grade teacher, suggests introducing webbing to students:

> Explain to students that the brain works in a very complex way. Certain thoughts, sounds, smells, tastes can trigger memories. No one else's brain can bring up exactly the same thoughts or memories as yours can. We can show others on paper how our brain works through webbing.

When Elane Murphy began a weather unit in her kindergarten class, she taped a large sheet of paper to the chalkboard. She wrote the word *weather* in the center of the paper. Students brainstormed different words that relate to weather. She recorded the words and had the children draw pictures to accompany the words. This became a class web as the children drew circles around the word-picture combinations and connected them to the central word: *weather*.

Each child received a book of twenty pages. Every day the students looked outside. They wrote the date at the top of a page, drew a picture describing what they thought the weather was like that day, and then copied a related word onto the page.

Some primary students benefit from more structured webbing. A template of spaces on a sheet of paper can be used to guide them. The example below is from a first-grade teacher.

The beauty of webbing lies in its randomness, yet for some that very freedom may be uncomfortable. If students seem daunted, have them use a half sheet of paper to start. Others lose their inhibitions if they web with felt markers or crayons.

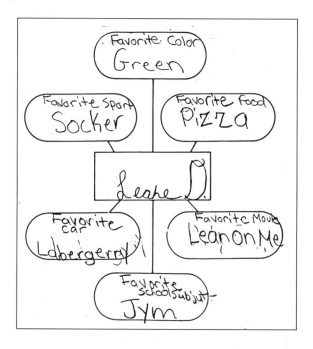

ALTERED POINT OF VIEW

Blending imagination with attention to detail or prior knowledge is the recipe for journal writing from an altered point of view. Students are asked to put themselves in the place of another human, animal, or thing and write in the first person. They may assume the personas of characters from fiction or history; some create fantasy beings. The results are often humorous, sometimes insightful, and at best illuminating. Journal entries can be in the form of free writing, lists, or webs.

Reading a story that has an unusual point of view models the approach. Lalo Mangaoang chose to read *The True Story of the Three Little Pigs!* by Jon Scieszka to his fourth-graders. This story tells the folk tale from the wolf's perspective. (He claims he was framed!)

After hearing and discussing the story, Lalo directed his students to choose another character from a folk tale and write in their journals from that character's point of view.

Class webbing based on a fictional or historical character is another way to begin. Choose a character and ask students to brainstorm. What does that character feel, see, and hear? What's important to him or her? Describe a typical day in this person's life. Record students' responses on the board.

Altered point of view can be adapted to different topics and grade levels. A class of intermediate students might split into groups and select individuals who have conflicting strong opinions of issues in history or literature. Students enjoy writing journal entries and then hearing "the opposition."

A primary class took a field trip to a pig farm and spent some time observing pigs. When they returned to class, they brainstormed what a pig's life is like. Then their teacher passed out paper with an outline of a pig, right, and students recorded their impressions in the first person.

I am a pig. I like to play and I am pink so when I go fast I bump into the fence and I can go fast but not very fast.

Students write about inanimate objects as well as living things, which encourages them to develop sensory awareness, imagination, and playfulness. They may choose something very common like a shoe, toy, book, or desk.

Altered points of view may be drawn from elements in a class web. The kindergarten students in Elane Murphy's class picked one element—"rainy"—from the class web and then wrote a class story from the raindrop's point of view.

Raindrop

I am a raindrop. My name is Sara. I live in a big gray cloud with all the other raindrops. I was growing bigger and bigger each day. One day I decided I wanted to leave the big gray cloud that had been my home for so long. I was big now and ready to go. I was in the center and worked my way to the edge and let go.

Some students are much more comfortable writing their altered points of view in list form. Both prose and list forms work well. Compare these two examples of a kite's point of view (original spelling maintained):

If I were a kite I would fly high in the ski and look down and I would see all sorts of people that would look like bugs. The trees would look like tall trees, the houce would looks like dice. I would see cars that drive on miniature racetrack. The grass would look like maps.

If I was a kite I would flay high in the air and look done and I would see the peple and look ant trees,
biiledings [buildings]
fair
gass stashons [gas stations]
store
dogs
cats
markes [markets]
school
montens [mountains]

Writing from an altered point of view is an effective way for elementary children to develop empathy, which requires stepping into another's shoes and considering what that person feels or thinks. Teachers have successfully used this strategy in resolving conflicts. When a dispute occurs between two students, after a cooling-off period each is asked to write a journal entry about the incident from the other's point of view. The insight gained from this exercise often eliminates further conflict.

UNSENT LETTERS

Like altered point of view, unsent letters promote empathy and draw on the imagination. Students address a specific individual and write in the first person using the principles of free writing. They may write personal letters to historical, imaginary, fictional, or real individuals. In their letters they freely express ideas and feelings, engage in fantasy, or work on personal issues.

Unsent letters are so called because they are seldom mailed. Their purpose is to record ideas, which are only shared with a teacher, a buddy, or parents. Exceptions occur when students find that they want to share their ideas with someone such as an author or a politician. In such cases the journal entries are considered first drafts and are revised and edited before being mailed.

A class of fourth-graders wrote letters during music appreciation time to composers and musicians they had studied. One student combined the unsent-letter and altered-point-of-view techniques, right.

> Nichola!
>
> My concert was cencasonal! The Royal Palace love it. The Queen of England wants me to play. I have no idea of what I should play. Well I'll write again. latter bye
>
> Nicole
>
> Dear Mom.
>
> I'm fine and I'm eating good the people here is nice to me. Prolly because I can play the piano. You know what I mean. The next concert is for children and it will be Twinkle, Twinkle little Star by Mozart, Mozart father.
>
> Niki

In a fifth-grade class the students wrote to a favorite author. One girl chose to address an unsent letter to Laura Ingalls Wilder, below.

Becca Larson
May 15
Writing

Dear Laura Ingalls Wilder,

I love your books. I bet it was hard during the Long Winter in De Smet.

It sounds like you liked your life.

What was your favorite time of your life?

Your Parents sound like really nice folks.

I would have loved to be your friend or sister.

Your Friend,
Becca Larson

Sometimes students will take the opportunity to write to a relative who has passed away or is no longer living with the child's family. This third-grader wrote to his grandfather:

> Dear Grandfather June,
> I know I never saw you befor.
> My mom told me a lot about
> you and how you died. I wish
> you were still alive so I could
> see you. my mom wishes she
> can see you to.

Unsent letters give students opportunities to explore ideas or emotions while they practice the conventions of letter writing. They have a wide range of applications.

CLOSE OBSERVATION

The technique of close observation is time-honored in journal writing. Throughout history naturalists, explorers, and ordinary travelers have recorded their observations of the sights, sounds, and smells of exotic places. Others, such as Thoreau, studied and recorded changes in their own backyards. Important to close observation is using all five senses (sight, hearing, smell, taste, and touch) to incorporate sensory detail into a journal entry.

Close observation is really descriptive writing. When it is done well, the writer follows the maxim to "show not tell" in recreating a scene or experience. Therefore, when you model the technique, demonstrate the difference between writing "Our teacher is very happy today" and "Our teacher had a big smile on her face when we came in today. She laughed at everything."

To help students remember to use all their senses, some teachers provide a list of prompts, such as the following:

I see…
I hear…
I touch…
I smell…
I taste…

As an extension, students add reflective comments by observing their feelings. Does the item or scene evoke an emotion or remind them of something else? What related ideas does it inspire? In this way they observe an interior as well as an exterior environment. To facilitate this intro-spection, these prompts could be added to the list:

I think…
I feel…
I remember…

Often close-observation writing is preceded by a field trip or a simple excursion like a walk around the playground. At other times you may ask students to remain in their seats and make observations of objects that they are able to feel. For example, you might pass around a basket of stones or shells and have each of the children choose one to describe in their journals.

Another classic use of close observation is a scientific log. You may ask students to log their observations of a science project—watching a seed grow, for example. Such a log works well as a separate journal kept during the life of an experiment.

Making notes of the world around them is a good centering exercise to increase students' awareness and bring them into the here and now. Focusing on the minute details of the immediate surroundings keeps the writer's mind from wandering and is a useful way to settle down a group that is excited or agitated. In response to the complaint "I don't know what to write," suggest that the student write about what he or she observes then and there.

In Joan Lew's second-grade class, Miriam sat staring at her journal while her classmates drew pictures of their houses and listed the colors and smells they remembered. Joan knelt by Miriam's desk and asked, "Do you have a question about the journal topic?"

Miriam answered, "I don't know what to write."

Joan made sure that she had Miriam's attention and said, "Look around our classroom. What colors do you see?"

Miriam looked at the walls. "I see blue. Red. Green. Purplish red."

"Good," encouraged the teacher. "Write those down on your paper." Miriam listed the colors, adding yellow and orange.

"What else do you see in the room?"

Miriam looked around again. "Desks, kids, plants."

"I like the things you are noticing. Will you draw a picture of our room?"

By the time Joan made this suggestion, Miriam was drawing the outline of the classroom. The teacher added further reinforcement and then left to encourage other journalers by making factual comments about their entries.

One third-grade teacher asked her students to observe pictures of cats and then make journal entries to record their observations. She extended the activity by having volunteers read their journal entries and then asking the rest of the class to guess which cat was being described.

Here are some other observation possibilities that range from the minute to the grand:

> CHANGEY   1
> 2-22-91
> writing
>
>   I have greenish brown
> eyes, And a lot of fur. I am
> orange. I am on the grass, and
> am staring. You can barly notes my
> ears, I have so much fur.
>
> You are right. You can barely
> notice your ears due to so much
> fur.

- ✐ Look carefully at a small area of grass.

- ✐ Examine an orange.

⌀ Describe a piece of art.

⌀ Convey the atmosphere of a science fair or an assembly.

If you like students to share their journal writing occasionally, close-observation entries are good ones to read aloud. Because they are less personal, students are more comfortable letting others hear what they have written. One of the valuable outcomes of this kind of sharing is to hear how each writer's observations of the same object or place differ. Once again we are reminded that each of us brings a unique perspective to our writing. Another benefit to reading entries aloud is that children practice and gain confidence in speaking before others.

ME-MAPS AND DRAWING

Many primary children typically draw pictures or designs and then write about their drawings. Me-maps—non-verbal entries—are a kind of drawing especially appropriate to journals. They incorporate pictures and symbols to record thoughts, ideas, and feelings. In this technique, finding a way to express ideas without words is more important than artistic ability. Me-maps combine the freedom of webbing with the satisfaction of doodling.

To guide students in learning the technique, create your own me-map on the overhead or chalkboard. Me-maps center on the individual. Like webbing, the process begins with a blank piece of paper. Children draw pictures of themselves or use symbols such as a book, a bird, or a bicycle.

Next, have the students draw objects or individuals that are important or meaningful to them. Children often draw pictures of food, school, family, friends, and toys. Pizza and ice cream appear in many me-maps. The focus of the rest of the map may take many forms, ranging from how students feel to plans for a family vacation. The illustration below shows a me-map done by a third-grader.

With assistance, even kindergarten students can draw me-maps. The example shown below was drawn on a 12-by-18 inch (30 cm-by-48 cm) piece of paper using a felt pen.

The concept of me-maps can be expanded beyond the individual to the rest of the environment. For example, students often enjoy drawing floor plans of

their houses, below, or maps of their neighborhoods. Intermediate students draw me-maps to illustrate things they have seen on field trips.

Teachers often ask how me-maps are different from just "drawing pictures." Me-maps focus on the individual or the individual's environment. Drawing may accompany any form of journal entry, particularly in the primary grades. As students develop, their drawings usually become more illustrative and less central to their expression. Students who continue to limit their journal entries only to drawings or me-maps should be asked to write a minimum number of words or sentences per day.

Me-maps promote creativity and foster attention to detail. Many students report that they find me-maps the most fun of all the journal techniques.

CONCLUDING THOUGHTS

You will undoubtedly develop your own adaptations to these standard techniques. Introduce each of the techniques over time. Provide opportunities for practicing each one before going on to another. Begin with free writing, listing, and webbing, which need to be taught before going on to other techniques. Free writing is the basis for unsent letters and altered points of view. Listing and webbing are useful for brainstorming ideas as well as for journal entries. Remember to allow the right brain free rein every now and then and assign me-maps at intervals.

All these techniques can be used effectively in individual journals. With some explanation to set the scene, they can be applied to dialogue and buddy journals as well. Learning logs are generally limited to focused free writing, listing, and webbing. Even though you may personally prefer one technique or type, remember that one is not inherently better than another; the choice is a matter of taste and style. To catch the largest number of fish, cast your net as widely as possible. Vary your assignments.

Every journey begins with some planning, and introducing journal writing in your classroom is no exception. Establishing the purpose, gathering the tools, and determining the guidelines will help you develop clear expectations for the trip ahead.

As you work with various types of journals and techniques, you will find the ones that suit your classroom best. We have noticed that individuals often feel more comfortable with one type of journal or technique over another. A student who loves buddy journals may also complete individual entries, but not particularly enjoy the process. Another may want to spend an entire journaling period working on a learning log, but not want to share anything in a dialogue journal. The same kinds of experience may well be true for you.

Pick and choose the ideas presented in this book that are appropriate to your needs. Each journaling unit in each classroom will be a unique blend of types and techniques, based on both the teacher's and students' needs and preferences.

We suggest that you begin a personal journal before introducing the curriculum. Spend some time free writing about your purpose and the goals for your students. Try some sentence starters like the following:

- Journals are important because…
- I like journaling because…
- I want my students to gain…from their journals.
- At the end of the year, my students will have learned…
- I am willing to commit…to make journals work.

Four elementary teachers were excited about starting to use journals after taking a weekend class at a local university. They decided to meet after school and put their new-found knowledge into practice. Each started a journal by responding to the prompts suggested above and then brought these musings to a meeting. After they clarified some of their goals, they developed guidelines that defined specific expectations and established an approach that would work for them and their students. (Guidelines are also a useful tool for explaining your mission statement to parents, colleagues, and administrators.)

The teachers reviewed the brainstorming techniques they had learned (free writing, listing, webbing) and decided to make a list. They started with "classroom journals" and called out ideas that would work for the students in their particular grade levels and settings, as well as with their curriculum requirements. One of the teachers recorded all the ideas on the chalkboard. Some were questions:

- What kind of journals shall we start with?
- How long shall the unit be?
- How often will students write in them? All year?
- What will they write in? Notebooks? Their binders?
- Will students write daily? Twice weekly?

Some already had ideas of what they wanted to do:

- I'll start with free writing.
- I'll make monthly team journals.
- I'll read all journals weekly.
- Buddy journals sound like fun.

Working from their list, they refined their ideas and established guidelines under the following headings:

- mission statement
- confidentiality
- topics (student-selected or provided by teacher?)
- evaluation/grading

 ✐ sharing with others
 ✐ dialogue journals?
 ✐ logistics

Before ending their meeting, they agreed to meet again in a month and re-evaluate the effectiveness of their guidelines.

Before having a similar discussion in your school, read the rest of this chapter, which discusses the guideline items in more depth. Like any good list of rules, they should be simple and take no more than one page.

MISSION STATEMENT

A mission statement will help you stay focused on the purpose of the activity as the year progresses. It articulates goals and explains your reasons for incorporating the use of journals into your curriculum. Developing a mission statement will help you clarify your goals into a final, public form. It also serves as a rationale that you can share with your students, parents, colleagues, and administrators. In your mission statement explain clearly why you are using this approach to writing in your classroom. For example, you might explain that writing and thinking are like any other skills: improvement only comes with practice, and the more you practice, the better you get.

Stacy Wood suggested a seven-point mission statement:

The purpose of journals is to

1. expand students' vocabularies;

2. increase the desire to write clearly to express ideas, emotions, revelations, and observations;

3. help students solve their own problems by hashing them out on paper;

4. precipitate behavior changes (writing about behavior can help alter it; journals help students see themselves from a different point of view);

5. sharpen note-taking skills to keep up with the brain's synapses during a furious stream of writing;

6. remind students of accomplishments that they may forget;

7. create a dialogue not only between the student and teacher but also between the student and his or her own inner thoughts and feelings.

Send your journaling guidelines home with students so their parents and guardians will get an idea of the breadth of the program.

SCHEDULING

An important initial decision is to decide how often students will write in their journals. Ideally, journaling will become part of the daily classroom routine, although daily journaling is not appropriate for every class. If it seems appropriate for your class, try to build up to having students write in their journals daily. You may begin by having them write twice weekly, say on Tuesday and Thursday. Then, when that becomes comfortable, add another day.

When you begin journaling, set a consistent time of day for the activity. Some programs set aside the first twenty to thirty minutes of the morning, others the last part of the afternoon. At the beginning of the year, the time of day is not as important as consistency. Later in the year, when students are used to journal writing, you may ask them to write at other times. For example, during a social studies unit, Orene Crabtree asks her students to pull out their journals and write about life from the point of view of an explorer who is searching for the source of the Nile River. Later that day she asks them to use their journals again to respond to a piece of music using close observation.

You will want to check students' journal entries on a regular basis. Handling this task in an effective manner is important to establishing journal writing as part of your curriculum. If blossoming journal writers receive no feedback, their interest wanes quickly. You can respond with verbal or written comments, using stick-on notes, stamps, stickers, or in conferences.

You may promise to read journals daily only to find that it takes three hours instead of one. Another alternative is to read the journals weekly. No matter how much you enjoy reading the journals, if you have twenty-five students making daily journal entries, you will be reading 125 entries each weekend. This is one of the traps many teachers set for themselves: making unrealistic demands on their own time. Reading journals every day is not necessary. Students' motivation can come from sharing with a buddy or simply from seeing the quantity of their entries increase. One goal of journaling is to build independent writers, and we encourage you to do that by giving support and feedback in a way that allows students to become self-motivated.

If you want to limit the time spent reading journals, you can ask students to star one entry per week for you to read. This will reduce the number of journals you are committed to reading from 125 to 25. Another possibility is to collect journals from a different group of the class each week. If you are using dialogue journals, triple your planned response time.

Think realistically about how often you want students to write and how often you will respond, and let them know the expectations before they begin. The most successful journal programs combine a strong backbone of structure with creative, intellectually stimulating writing activities.

CONFIDENTIALITY

Who will read students' journal entries and under what circumstances? For many teachers, the response to this question is simple: no one but the teacher is ever to see student journals. If the journals are to be shared with others, some teachers suggest to their students that they not write private thoughts, as their journals will be shared freely with classmates and parents as well as the teacher. Others give students the option of writing some entries they don't want shared. They are asked to fold those pages over to identify them as such. The teacher must then respect the student's wish for privacy.

Some confidential journal entries may be of a private nature, while others may be explorations about classroom readings or discussions that a student is not ready to share. Respecting students' rights is paramount if they are to record their thoughts, ideas, and feelings freely. If you say that a journal is totally confidential except for your occasional checking, and that promise is broken, the student will feel betrayed by this breach of trust.

Remember that journaling in a classroom is different from writing in a diary at home. In some exceptional situations, under some conditions, other adults besides the teacher have the right to access student journals. These adults could be teachers, health professionals, or parents. It is only fair to let students know that others may be privy to their writing or to information they have recorded if the teacher believes their safety is at risk. Without going into the legal ramifications, you can tell students that you have a responsibility to be sure they are safe. Therefore, if you believe they are in any danger, you will take action to protect them.

For some students the journal is a safe place to process pain in their lives or an avenue to seek help from a trusted teacher. A few students have reported abuse or suicidal thoughts, and these entries can only be interpreted as cries for help. For those in the helping professions such as education and medicine, those calls must be heeded, and many states and provinces have legal requirements to report suspected abuse.

When you read journals, attend to what students may be trying to tell you. Young people often use journals as a forum for communicating requests as well as for exploring thoughts and experiences in both their personal and academic lives.

PARENTS' INVOLVEMENT

Parents are often interested in their children's journals and may ask to see them during teacher–parent conferences. Many teachers send letters and a copy of the guidelines home with the children to explain the purpose that journals have in the classroom (below). This letter can clarify if the journals will—or will not—be made available

---

Dear Parent:

   I am excited that our fourth-grade class will be using journals this year. Journals give students a place to practice writing and explore the concepts we cover in language, science, math, and social studies.

   We will use several types of journals, including learning logs, dialogue journals, and buddy journals. We will begin with dialogue journals and would like you to participate. In dialogue journals students write and an adult responds in writing. The result is a written conversation.

   The students will write in their journals on Monday, and I will respond by Wednesday. They will write again on Thursday and include a question for you to answer. Please write a response in your son's or daughter's journal when he or she brings it to you on [date]. Students will be writing to you each Thursday during the month of [name of month].

   You may notice some errors in spelling or grammar in the journal entries. Rather than mark them, I use the mistaken words or mechanics correctly when I write back. For example, if a child writes the word *whether* when the context is about weather, I am sure to use the word *weather* in my response. This method of correction emphasizes the things the students are doing right rather than those they are doing wrong and helps students improve their spelling and grammar.

   I will have your child's journal available at our fall conference for you to look at. If you have any questions before then, please call me at [telephone number].

Sincerely,

to parents. If they are to be shared with parents, this can lead to a journaling partnership among you, your students, and their parents.

If you choose to use dialogue journals and develop a written conversation between you and a student, think about including the parent as another partner in the conversation. In this case have the children ask their parents a question in the journals. Keep the initial questions at the descriptive level of response to encourage parents to recall and describe: What was school like when you were in second grade? Tell me why you like your favorite music. Tell me about your favorite children's story? This process gives parents an opportunity to share something about their own childhood and interests with their children. Parents' enthusiasm can increase students' commitment to journaling.

TOPICS

Students who have written in journals before come to your classroom with a preconceived idea about what to write, while those who are writing in journals for the first time may feel uncomfortable until they have been given a specific topic. In your guidelines specify whether or not topics are to be teacher-provided or self-selected.

As with the introduction of any new activity, more guidance is needed at the beginning of the process. Before your first journaling day, develop a list of appropriate topics and place them in a conspicuous place in the front of the room. For the first few journaling sessions, have students choose a topic from the list. The following all-purpose "list of lists" is provided as a starting point:

- People I love
- People who have had special influence on me
- What I'm most proud of
- The best times in my life
- The worst times in my life

- Firsts (first day of school, first tooth, first…)
- Teachers/schools
- Clubs/teams/sports/hobbies
- Favorite objects (such as clothing, a toy, a blanket)
- Favorites in endless categories (such as music, books, food, video games)
- Pets
- Vacations
- Things I love to do
- Times I have needed courage
- What I'd do to change the world (or school, or my parents)

After students gain experience in journaling and become more confident, they tend to write more often on topics of their own choice.

Roy Nakagawa asks his third-graders to brainstorm ideas for journal topics. Immediately, fifteen hands wave in the air. He records their suggestions on a large sheet of paper: movies, bugs, superheroes, fun games to play. For the next few weeks, students refer to the list hanging on the wall when they ponder what to write about.

The final step to independent journal writing is for small groups or partners to brainstorm their own lists of topics. A good place to keep such lists is the inside covers of students' journals. Often lists may be inspired by class readings, field trips, or discussions.

Using the model list of lists, both primary and intermediate teachers have developed their own lists to post in their classrooms for students to refer to. The following are examples for each level.

A Primary List of Lists
- School helpers
- School rules
- Responsibilities
- Things I do well

- Favorite things to do with grandma/grandpa/mom/dad/brother/sister
- What to do after school
- Favorite jokes
- Things that go up and down
- Why I get mad
- Things to kick
- Hiding places

An Intermediate Lists of Lists
- Times I was scared/happy/sad/confused
- Dreams
- What I could be when I grow up
- Favorite memories
- Things I do well/do not do so well/would like to do well
- Things to take camping
- What I like in a teacher/friend/brother/sister
- Things I can recycle
- What causes stress?
- Things to do around the house
- Yummers and yuckers
- Types of weird sandwiches
- Manners

Sentence starters—open-ended phrases that prompt students' entries—are another good way to begin journals. The following are some samples:

- If I had a million dollars…
- The best day in my life was…
- If I were a blue jay, I would…
- If I could live anywhere in the world, I would live…
- John McFee was…because…

A third way to introduce journals is to present topics from books that list writing ideas or children's questions. Several books include a variety of topics and questions appropriate for kindergarten to grade six. The following are two questions from *The Kids' Book of Questions* (Stock 1988):

> ✐ If you could have your room clean and neat all the time or jumbled and messy, which would you prefer?

> ✐ Have you ever—without telling anyone—let someone beat you at a game you could easily have won? If so, why?

We certainly would not discourage students from writing on topics of their own choice. In fact, teachers often disagree about the advisability of assigning topics. At one end of the spectrum are those who say that the best writing grows naturally out of students' experiences. They believe that students have a higher level of ownership and responsibility for writing that they originate and that "canned" topics squelch their enthusiasm (Calkins 1986). Other teachers feel strongly that they need to help students generate topic lists so that no student can say, "I don't know what to write." Other teachers choose topics and structure students' writing to address specific skills.

EVALUATION

How do you hold students accountable for their journal writing? Will their journaling efforts be factored into grades on their report cards? Will students choose entries to put into portfolios?

Including journals as part of a student's grade creates more incentive for some students to write, and many teachers want a way to record journaling efforts in their grade books. However, students' journaling voices, tones, and styles are unique, and teachers struggle to come up with a quantifiable means of determining grades for journaling.

The grading issue can be approached in several ways. One effective and simple method to give students credit for their journal writing is to assign points for entries made. Perhaps each day's entry will be worth one point. You would then note five points for five days' worth of entries.

If you choose to use this system, establish and communicate to students the basic criteria of exactly what constitutes "an entry." Most entries are a form of narrative: altered point of view, unsent letters, learning logs, buddy journals. They can be quantified by number of lines or words, even though this does not measure the quality of the expression. Me-maps, webs, and drawings fall into a different category, but can also be quantified by their extent.

A point system is the most easily understood criterion. A similar procedure is to use a check-plus-minus system. In this case an entry that is exceptional for its length or the quality of the thinking it reflects receives a plus; an "average" entry receives a check; and a minimal or hasty entry receives a minus.

Another approach to monitoring journals in intermediate grades is to observe and record whether or not students are working during journal writing time. You observe that students are actually writing during the appointed time, but you do not attempt to collect their journals and check off entries. Every few weeks you ask students to summarize their journals. This may be done with a journal evaluation form on which students record specific types of phrases or entries (for example, three sensory details from a close observation of a place; a typical entry; an atypical entry). Another option is to ask students to prepare a table of contents of their journal entries. You can review the table of contents and make a judgment about the kind of writing the student has been doing. With either of these systems, the student's grade is based on the summary that the student prepares in class (Countryman 1992; Sullivan 1989).

Yet another option is for students to choose one journal entry a week and add it to a writing portfolio. If students add just one piece of writing to their portfolios every other week during a school year, they will have eighteen by mid-June. They can then compare a piece of September's writing with a piece of June's and see how far they have grown in writing skill development, subject area knowledge, or both. Perspective and comparison are powerful tools in understanding growth as learners.

Some teachers choose not to grade journals at all, but ask students to use journal entries as a basis for further work that *will* be evaluated. In his fourth-grade class, Darren has been journaling about the Underground Railroad. He's taken the altered points of view of Harriet Tubman; of Garrett, a man who sheltered runaways; and of Isaiah, a young boy who is hiding in Garrett's barn. Darren chooses to polish his journal entry about Isaiah. He rewrites it in his notebook, this time adding an introduction and conclusion. He asks Sue Anne, his classmate, to check his spelling. On Friday Darren reads the polished altered point of view to his class. Teacher Pat Guild bases Darren's grade on his oral presentation.

In other classes learning logs become the storehouse for systematic observations that are later included in a science report. For example, Rosa has been noting the growth of seedlings in her learning log. She rereads her entries, then summarizes her observations in a report that she puts into her science portfolio. In some classes a cumulative record of physical education activities is included in a final personal fitness report; team journal entries become part of the overall grade for a group project or report; a student uses close observations he's written about a piece of music as the impetus for a poem.

SHARING WITH OTHERS

Dialogue, buddy, and team journals are designed to be shared with at least one other person. Altered points of view, webs, lists, unsent letters, close observations, me-maps, free writing, and learning logs in all types of journals may be shared from time to time.

In one school, first- and second-grade teachers arranged for their students to be buddies with each other. The children insisted that the two teachers also write back and forth to each other. Tammy Swant, one of the teachers, commented:

> The first-graders are motivated to write to second-graders because they are older. The second-graders are motivated to write to first-graders because they are going to teach them things like where to put periods.

If students are expected to share their journals with another student or the entire class, let them know in the guidelines what is expected. For example: "Each Friday you will choose one piece of free writing and read it to the class" or "On a regular basis, you will share one of your journal entries with your seat mate."

Teachers report that most students enjoy reading their work aloud. Even those who are shy or lacking confidence may be inspired to read after hearing their classmates' stories. For students with preferences for auditory learning, the sharing motivates them to write more. In some classrooms, students trade journals to read during sustained silent reading (SSR).

Sharing journal entries builds a journaling community as students get to know each other. And the more students find that their writing is accepted by others, the more confident they become.

DIALOGUE JOURNALS

We include dialogue journals—in which you have ongoing communication with your students—in the guidelines because the use of this kind of journal represents an important commitment. We want you to think about it carefully and then let students know how dialogue journals will be structured. The logistics of dialogue journals are discussed in chapter 2.

LOGISTICS

What will students write in?

Both the grade level and purpose will influence the physical nature of the journal chosen. Of the many formats described below, some are more appropriate for kindergarten and others for older primary and higher grades.

Very young children may write or draw journal entries on individual pieces of paper that are stored in pocket folders. This allows teachers the flexibility of providing as many sheets of paper as they wish.

Another option for primary students is to build one-week or two-week journals by stapling the appropriate number of pages into a construction-paper folder. The format may be large or small. A similar option is to have students decorate manila folders with drawings, paintings, or collages, which are then laminated. Punch three holes in one side, then assemble them with yarn or brads. This allows you to add or remove pages. Older students typically use spiral-bound notebooks.

Many primary teachers have had great success in using a big-book format, which allows children to draw on large surfaces. Others create covers that correspond to a theme or topic. For example, one kindergarten teacher cut orange construction-paper covers in the shape of pumpkins. The children drew or painted jack-o'-lantern faces on the front of their journals. On the pages inside, they responded to specific questions or dictated stories about pumpkins. Other themes that year included a September journal in the shape of a leaf and an April journal in the shape of a tulip.

Allow class time for older students to decorate the covers of their journals with a collage that represents them or an appropriate theme. This encourages even reluctant journalers to establish ownership. Remember that many students respond strongly to color and texture. Give them the option of using colored pens, as well as different colors and sizes of paper. As you can see, journals take many forms.

What if students want to journal on computers?

If your school is one of the many schools that have computer labs or classrooms with one or two computers available, we would encourage you to experiment by combining journaling and technology. Journals offer an authentic way for students to practice their word-processing skills. If a journal entry becomes the first step in the writing process, students may revise directly on the screen. Those who are beginning computer users and reluctant writers may be motivated to write by seeing the screen fill up with lines of words.

Students gain in several ways by using computer journals. Their keyboarding skills improve, but keep in mind that computer journaling can be frustrating if students have not mastered touch typing. Computer journaling also helps students who suffer from auditory dyslexia because they don't have to form the letters; they just have to choose them from the keyboard.

Where to keep them?

Keep journals in a safe place in the classroom. Some teachers choose a locked cabinet; others have a journal box or shelf visible in the classroom. Whichever your preference, be sure you can monitor access. Since journals may contain personal thoughts, feelings, or introspections, they need a bit of protection.

Some teachers choose to have students keep their journals in their desks. This works well as long as students don't take them home "by accident" or other students don't share their desks for different subjects.

SAMPLE GUIDELINES

The following are three sets of guidelines developed by teachers Marcene DuBois (grade two), Opal Oss (grade five), and Janine Brodine (grade six).

Guidelines for a Second-Grade Class

Mission statement

> Journal writing is an opportunity for students to express their feelings, thoughts, and ideas on a variety of topics or just to be free to be themselves.

Frequency

> Students will write two or three times a week at first. This may be increased to daily entries.

Confidentiality

> No one will read student journals but me. Sometimes I may ask a student's permission to read an entry orally. If there is something I think needs to be shared with others, I will discuss it with the student.

Topics

> Students will keep a list of topics in their desks, and I will usually allow them free choice. Occasionally, I will assign a topic.

Evaluation

> I will not give a letter grade for journal entries, but will use journals as a basis for the evaluation of written expression.

Sharing with others

> I will ask students to share orally one journal entry every two weeks. This is an excellent opportunity for students to work on grammar, sentence structure, and meaning.

Dialogue

> I will dialogue by using positive responses, words of encouragement, or a personal response to whatever students have written.

Logistics

Students will write in booklets made from lined printing paper with a construction-paper cover.

Guidelines for a Fifth-Grade Class

Mission statement

Journals give students a safe way to communicate and a good way to think out ideas, solutions, and plans. They provide a method to release frustration. Journaling is an excellent way to improve writing skills, as students learn to write by writing.

Frequency

Each day students will write in their journals from 9:00 to 9:15. I will write the next day's topic question or topic statement on the board just before the students are dismissed each day so that they can think about it during the evening and will be ready to write the next morning.

Confidentiality

Journals will be read by the individual student and the teacher only. Students may choose one entry (or more if desired) every two weeks to be shared with their parents. They will label those entries with a *P*, copy them, and place them in a secure place until conference time.

Topics

Both the students and I will generate topics. During the first two to three weeks, I will generate lists of topics, and children will generate ideas in their own journals to refer to at a later date. Later on I will provide the topics four days a week, and the students will choose their own on Friday.

Evaluation

Evaluation will begin after two weeks of journaling. Entries will be graded on their content and the amount of writing done. A ten-points-a-week system will be used. One-half page of good writing will be worth two points; less than one-half will be worth one point; no points will be awarded if writing quality is poor.

Sharing

Entries will be shared on a volunteer basis on Fridays. However, if several students want to do so, everyone will be invited to share during the week so that anyone who wants to has a chance to participate.

Dialogue

I will dialogue with students once a week in their journals. I will respond only to starred entries, although all entries will be read. I will write to four to five students each day and will have dialogued with every student by the end of the week.

Logistics

Students will write in self-designed notebooks.

Computer Journal Guidelines for a Sixth-Grade Class

Guidelines for Apple-Journals in the Summer Science Program

Mission statement

Apple-journals provide a means of practicing Appleworks skills and applying summer science experiences and concepts to other aspects of your life. The questions and answers below provide guidelines.

What is an Apple-journal?

An Apple-journal includes

- ideas about science activities;
- explorations of ideas, problems,
- reactions to field trips and readings;
- your feelings and experiences.

How should I write?

- Write freely and take risks.
- Content and exploration are most important.

✐ Don't worry about correct spelling, grammar, or sentences.

✐ Use your personal voice.

When should I write?

✐ Write every Monday through Friday for ten minutes at the beginning of each day.

How much should I write?

✐ Write a minimum of three lines daily, a maximum of one page.

Where do I keep my journal?

✐ Keep your journal on a personalized floppy disk to be kept in the classroom.

What should I write about?

✐ The daily topic suggestion will be in the master computer. Copy the file with the current date onto your disk. You can respond to the suggested topic or write about something of your own choosing.

Who will read my journal?

✐ The Appleworks instructor will read all journals on Tuesday and Thursday. She will respond in dialogue-journal form to questions. She may share questions or concerns with other instructors, but will not print out hard copies of your entries without your permission.

How will my journal be graded?

✐ If you write a minimum of three lines, you get a check. Less than that is a minus. Journals will make up 10 percent of your science grade.

5

In schools in which writing is a priority, classroom teachers who teach the core subject areas and specialists in music, art, and physical education work together to provide writing experiences in every subject. And educators who agree that writing is an important avenue to understanding make widespread use of journals as a teaching tool:

> Teaching *with* writing promotes student-centered learning: quite simply, the more students write in every class, the more they express themselves and take an active role in their own education—and the less, by implication, they depend on the teacher to tell them what to think and know. (Fulwiler 1986)

All the types of journals and journaling techniques discussed in chapters 2 and 3 can be used throughout the curriculum, although, as we have said before, not all techniques are applied in the same way at every grade level. Among the ways in which teachers can employ journals in their classrooms are the use of

- listing and webbing as forms of notetaking and summarizing;

- free writing and me-maps as avenues for students to show they understand the significance of what they learned;

- altered point of view and unsent letters as alternative methods for students to write "reports."

When teachers read students' daily journal writing, they have an accurate way to monitor learning. They also glean valuable clues as to ways in which their instruction can be improved.

Another advantage of using journals in all content areas is to broaden the role of writing beyond existing practices:

> If [writing activities] are used simply as tests of memory of materials presented by teacher or textbook, the role of writing in the development of higher order thinking skills will be short-circuited.
>
> For a variety of reasons, current models of instruction emphasize writing-as-recitation much more than they emphasize writing as a way of thinking about complex ideas. This is particularly true in subjects other than English.
> (Langer and Applebee 1985)

Anxiety blocks learning and consumes students' and, ultimately, the teacher's energy. Such a block may take the form of a *writing* block, but is actually a *thinking* block. When students explore a range of thinking skills, they discover the questions they need to ask themselves and their teacher.

Many teachers use the six classifications of Bloom's Taxonomy as a reminder to include opportunities for all levels of thinking: knowledge, comprehension, application, analysis, synthesis, and evaluation. With this as a guide for lesson planning, teachers may ask students to

- recall information or define science concepts;
- compare or discuss historical figures;
- illustrate sports rules;
- analyze the ingredients in a recipe;
- organize prewriting and draft a five-paragraph essay;
- criticize a clay sculpture.

These are just a few of the possible applications. When journals are used across the curriculum, students bring their best thinking to every subject.

Bloom's Taxonomy of the Cognitive Domain

As you plan lessons using this taxonomy, keep the following verbs in mind:

Level I
    recall, name, identify, show, report, tell

Level II
    describe, express, summarize, identify, illustrate, report

Evaluation	Level VI
Synthesis	Level V
Analysis	Level IV
Application	Level III
Comprehension	Level II
Knowledge	Level I

Level III
    show, solve, practice, discuss, illustrate, explain

Level IV
    compare, relate, diagram, criticize, question, summarize

Level V
    plan, imagine, organize, design, propose, create

Level VI
    judge, rate, predict, choose, evaluate, criticize

For example, teachers report great success in helping students master mathematical concepts through regular journal writing:

As students write in their journals, they become more reflective, expressive mathematicians. As they participate in problem solving in cooperative groups, they begin to view problem solving as a creative, rewarding activity and learn to work together to solve problems. As they connect writing and cooperative problem solving with diverse mathematical skills and concepts, they move a step closer to valuing mathematics as a powerful way to understand the world around them. (Wadlington, Bitner, Partridge, and Austin 1992)

Over the years we have collected hundreds of ideas from elementary teachers on using journals in the content areas. The following are examples of prompts for language arts, math, art, social studies, foreign languages, science, health, and physical education. In addition, because we believe social skills must be learned in the same way as other skills, we have included some ideas for journaling techniques that address self-esteem and interpersonal communication.

We know that much of the writing in a typical classroom addresses only lower-level thinking skills. Activities such as fill-in-the-blanks worksheets and answering the questions at the end of the chapter usually ask students to recall, label, define, or repeat—all Level I (knowledge) skills. Yet one of our goals as teachers is to provide opportunities and instruction at all levels. The lists that follow include specific prompts for using journals at the higher levels—comprehension, application, analysis, synthesis, and evaluation—using a variety of techniques and types of journals.

LANGUAGE ARTS/LITERATURE

Free Writing

- Analyze a character in a story. What was he or she like?
- Discuss three characters from your reading whom you'd like to know better.

Listing

- Recall all the words you know that start with [*a letter*].
- Recall things that are red/orange/gray.
- Suggest solutions to a problem presented in a story.
- Identify the qualities you liked or did not like in a character from a story.

Webbing

    🖋 Describe something in the classroom. Use the words in your web to create a poem.

    🖋 Record the emotions you felt when you read or heard a story/chapter/scene.

Close Observation

    🖋 Compare a real setting you have observed to one in a story.

    🖋 Describe the changes that take place in a character in a play (for example, Scrooge in *A Christmas Carol*).

Altered Point of View

    🖋 Imagine you are a letter of the alphabet. What letter would you be and why?

    🖋 Design a journal entry as if you were a character in a book or a character from another era.

    🖋 Pretend you are an adjective. Who are your friends? What do you do?

Unsent Letters

    🖋 Ask an author about his or her writing.

    🖋 Ask a character in a book about some aspect of his or her life that interests you.

Me-maps / Drawing

    🖋 Draw a map of the neighborhood that a fictional character lived in.

    🖋 Analyze a character in a story by doing a me-map for that character.

Learning Logs

    🖋 Express your reactions to a particular poem.

Buddy Journals

    🖋 Share your reactions to a book the teacher is reading to the class and predict the outcome of the story.

MUSIC

Free Writing

        ✎ While you listen to music, free-write to illustrate any scene that comes to your mind.

        ✎ Create a story suggested by the music.

Listing

        ✎ Record descriptive words that come to mind when listening to a particular piece of music.

        ✎ Recall all the musical terms you know.

Webbing

        ✎ Review all the different ways to make music that you can think of.

        ✎ Categorize the instruments of an orchestra.

        ✎ Draw note values and symbols.

Altered Point of View

        ✎ Write as though you were the baton used by the conductor/an instrument/the composer.

Unsent Letters

        ✎ Write to your favorite instrument. Include questions about the music it plays and its relationship to other instruments.

Close Observation

        ✎ Imagine a place that a particular piece of music reminds you of and describe it in detail.

        ✎ Compare and contrast a buddy's reactions to the music.

Me-maps / Drawings

        ✎ Use colored pens to show the colors that various instruments remind you of.

        ✎ Draw a me-map or picture that expresses how a particular piece of music makes you feel.

MATH

Free Writing

    🖉 Write an equation for a line graph and then explain your equation in words.

    🖉 Describe fractions for a third-grader. (This is a task for older students.)

    🖉 Express how you feel about math—comfort or anxiety.

    🖉 Create a story about a math problem or about your favorite number.

    🖉 Reflect on the math you've learned since beginning school in grade one and write a math autobiography.

    🖉 Are boys better in math than girls? Why or why not?

Listing

    🖉 Identify things around your house (or the classroom) that are square/rectangular/circular/oval/triangular.

    🖉 List ten things that are sold in sets (socks, towels, and so on).

Webbing

    🖉 Record all the math words (or math processes) you know.

    🖉 Note down all the factors of one number.

    🖉 Record and share all the ways you use numbers.

Altered Point of View

    🖉 Predict what will happen to a coin or dollar bill when it leaves your hand.

    🖉 Pretend you are a number and write about your importance.

Unsent Letters

    🖉 Compose a letter to a famous mathematician criticizing or interpreting his or her theories.

    🖉 In a letter to a friend, illustrate and describe your favorite shape.

Me-maps / Drawing

 🖉 Illustrate a math process using only pictures.

 🖉 Draw the different ways a set of tangrams can be assembled.

Learning Logs

 🖉 Do a math problem on the left and explain your process on the right.

Buddy Journals

 🖉 Ask math questions and explain math concepts to each other.

 🖉 Did you ask a question in math today? Tell me about it. If you didn't, what question do you wish you'd asked?

SOCIAL STUDIES

Free Writing

 🖉 Write the log of an imaginary explorer.

 🖉 Predict the results if the circumstances of a particular event in history had been different (for example, Battle of the Alamo, assassination of Martin Luther King).

 🖉 Analyze a current political issue (for example, war, colonization, immigration, allocation of resources).

Webbing

 🖉 Compare and contrast areas (residential, business, industrial) of your town or city.

 🖉 Record the things that people needed to survive during a specific historical period.

 🖉 What do you already know about another country's foods/customs/clothing/culture?

Altered Point of View

 🖉 Imagine the daily life of a child your age in another culture.

 🖉 Put yourself in one of the pictures in your textbook. Describe what's going on around you.

Unsent Letters

- Write a letter to a politician criticizing his or her policy.
- Write a letter to an explorer evaluating his or her contributions.

Close Observation

- Using pictures, photos, or your mind's eye, describe a place you've visited on vacation.
- From a film or photographs, contrast a city in a foreign land to one in Canada or the United States.

Me-maps / Drawing

- Create a me-map that shows yourself in relation to your community (city, neighborhood, and so on)
- Draw a diagram of your classroom or the school grounds.
- Create a genealogy or family tree.
- Show ways in which you could be a community helper in your town or neighborhood.

Team Journals

- Create journals of ordinary people in another time or country. Record their daily routines or their descriptions of important events.

SCIENCE

Free Writing

- Propose and describe a useful invention.
- Explain gravity (or another similar concept).
- Describe your favorite phase of the moon.

Listing

- Name plants or animals that fly/growl/crawl/swim.
- Explore what-if questions. From a class list, choose one and answer it. (What if snakes could fly? What if the earth had three moons?)
- Classify plants/animals/rocks by size/color/shape/weight.

Webbing

 🖋 Record all the jobs you know about in the science field.

 🖋 Record all the living things that might be found in a given environment (sea, forest, and so on).

Close Observation

 🖋 Watch a seed grow and describe its appearance each day.

 🖋 Make a daily record of changes in the weather.

Altered Point of View

 🖋 From an animal's point of view, explain the effects of clear cutting a forest/draining wetlands.

 🖋 Imagine you are an alien from another planet interpreting earth.

 🖋 Summarize the life story of a seed.

 🖋 Imagine you are a neutron/star/mountain/grain of sand.

 🖋 Look fifty to one hundred years into the future and describe your city or surroundings.

Unsent Letters

 🖋 Write to Copernicus, Einstein, or another renowned scientist to tell him or her about the effect on the world of his or her work.

 🖋 Pretend you are an animal in the zoo. Give advice to the zoo keeper.

Me-maps / Drawing

 🖋 Diagram the steps you took to determine the outcome of an experiment.

 🖋 Illustrate the life of an animal living in a specific environment (rain forest, tundra, Antarctic).

Team Journals

 🖋 Log the growth of plants in your vegetable garden project.

 🖋 After walking together in a nearby park, discuss the types of plants/trees/insects.

HEALTH/PHYSICAL EDUCATION

Free Writing

- Keep a daily record of your physical exercise. Describe how you feel after exercising.
- Predict sports of the future.
- What would your life be like if you ate only junk food?

Webbing

- Plan the ideal playground for your school.
- Review the rules for tether ball/softball/hopscotch.
- Create a children's menu for your house or a restaurant.
- Classify the foods you normally eat according to the basic food groups.
- Recall all the bones/organs in the body.

Altered Point of View

- Describe the feelings of a player on a losing/winning team.
- Explore the game from the point of view of your or another's tennis shoe.
- Imagine yourself in five, ten, and twenty years if you smoke/use alcohol/use drugs.
- You are your stomach/lungs/other body part.

Close Observation

- Analyze how body parts are used during games and exercise.
- Find your pulse. Record what you feel, sense, think.
- Analyze a single game or period. What do you see, hear, smell, feel?

Me-maps/Drawing

- Show your personal eating habits.
- Illustrate your favorite foods.

Learning Logs

- List playground rules on the left and give your opinions of them on the right.

Team Journals

 ✐ Explore views on staying healthy (eating nutritious food, getting exercise, for example).

 ✐ Share feelings and observations with members of your soccer, basketball, or jump-rope team.

ART

Free Writing

 ✐ Describe how a painting makes you feel.

 ✐ Compare and contrast unlike things or beings (for example, trees to people, cars to birds, a swing to a sock).

Listing

 ✐ Brainstorm all the possible titles for a painting.

 ✐ Decide what materials are needed for a craft (knitting, for example).

Webbing

 ✐ Explore a color. For example, what does green make you think of?

 ✐ Recall the colors on a color wheel.

Altered Point of View

 ✐ Pretend you are a figure in a photograph or painting.

 ✐ Write as though you were a sculpture in a museum or park.

FOREIGN LANGUAGES

Free Writing

 ✐ As you progress, write more and more in the language you are studying. Increase the percentage of each entry written in French/Spanish/Japanese.

 ✐ Imagine you are a student from another country visiting this classroom. How would you feel?

Listing

- Name customs/foods found in a particular culture.
- What important words do you need to know in another country (*bathroom*, *hello*, *telephone*, for example)?
- Plan what to take on a trip to China/Argentina/Mali.
- Recall and record the words you already know in this language.
- Name other countries and their languages.

Webbing

- Compare our food/sports/schools to those of a country whose language you are studying.

Close Observation

- Give details of a food or object from a country in which the language you are studying is spoken.

Unsent Letters

- Discuss school (or any other topic) with a student your age in another country.

Dialogue or Buddy Journals

- Try out your new vocabulary.

SOCIAL SKILLS/PERSONAL GROWTH

Listing

- Outline your personal goals for the next day.
- Create your own set of rules and consequences for the school or classroom.

Altered Point of View

- Describe a conflict from the point of view of a student other than yourself.

Unsent Letters

- Write a letter to the principal.
- Write to a student just entering your grade. What must he or she do to succeed in this grade?

Me-maps / Drawing

  🖉 Diagram relationships in your family.

  🖉 Illustrate the importance of happiness (or another feeling) to your life.

  🖉 Plan goals to pursue a specific dream of yours.

Buddy Journals

  🖉 Share your thoughts and feelings about a conflict that happened at school.

Learning Logs

  🖉 Record your opinions about the school rules or disciplinary code.

CONCLUDING THOUGHTS

Some journal types are universal in application. Learning logs work well in all subject areas; use them to help students respond to reading or other learning tools. Similarly, dialogue journals can be used in any part of the curriculum to allow students to express their joys and frustrations with the subject matter.

  Don't forget that journals are good ways for you to get feedback in any subject area. Have your students use starter sentences such as the following:

  🖉 My biggest question about this lesson is...

  🖉 I thought this test was...

  🖉 My biggest worry about this class is...

  🖉 What is really hard/easy about this is...

  🖉 I need to tell you [*teacher, study buddy*] that...

  🖉 Here's what I already know about this unit...

  🖉 Today I learned...

Regular, guided journal writing encourages students to use higher-level thinking skills. As students write and reflect on classroom experiences, they will *own* their responses and the processes that led to them. Their journals will also become repositories for their accumulated thoughts as well as immediate records of their reactions to learning.

6

Incorporating journals into a classroom is a process. It typically takes two or three years of experimentation with journals to work out the bugs. This chapter contains practical suggestions and advice for those starting journals for the first time. The chapter begins with a description of journaling in a school in which journals are used at every grade level. It then provides examples of unit and lesson plans that a number of teachers have used successfully.

LESSONS, ACTIVITIES, AND UNIT PLANS

Most teachers at Kimball Elementary School use journals in their classrooms. As you will see, the types of journals vary widely, but the teachers are unanimous in their commitment to the process.

Drawing primarily on a list of sight words, first-grade teachers post a "Word of the Day." Students are asked to use the word in a sentence in their journals. In the journal entry, right, the word of the day was *you*.

As the year progresses, students are encouraged to increase the number of sentences in each entry. Once a month, the children select one journal entry to be placed in their portfolios.

The first-graders are expected to explain why they selected a particular entry for their portfolios. At first they select entries because they like the subject. "I love cats,"

> Who are you?!
> What do you
> want? 3-16-94

a child says about the writing she chose. By spring many evaluate their entries and pick one because "I did a good job of writing on this."

In grade two, teachers use a calendar with a different writing prompt for each day. Their goal is to have students write at least four sentences daily. Every two weeks students are asked to select an entry to read to the entire class. In the journal entry below the prompt for the day was "Suddenly, the hands on the clock began to..."

The third-grade teachers use a variety of journals. In one classroom, the teacher uses journals primarily as responses to literature. In this classroom students select one of their journal entries to read for their video portfolio. In the same classroom, if students miss school to take a trip, they are expected to keep a detailed journal and share it with the class on their return. Students not only write in these travel journals but also include postcards, photos, and other memorabilia. In another classroom students start the day by writing in their journals for fifteen minutes. They generally produce about a page of writing in their spiral notebooks. Topics are generated by the students, who are encouraged to reflect on daily occurrences and to document their lives. Students often get ideas for topics from reading classmates' journals and continually add to their topic lists. In the example on the next page the student had listed topics on the first page of her journal. The entry was written based on one topic from the list: *accidents*.

In grade four students use math learning logs in several ways. Before the lesson starts, they do math warm-ups using math skills they have already learned. They record different terms and processes and then write about them in their own words or draw pictures to illustrate

Heather Swanson
April 11, 1994
Suddenly, the hands on the clock
began to... go backwards. The clock
took me back in time! I saw
dinosaurs! Then the clock's hand started
going forward agian. Then I was back
at home.

Journal Writing Ideas
Sports
Pets
Family
Birthdays
Accidents
Friends
School
vacations
scary stuff
Nature
Hot tub
Poeing
Places
TV shows
People

The Accident

1-25-94 One day I was up at my church camp. Then My dad's friend Terry came in to the lodge and said that Pete got in a car accident. Pete has two kids, Clar and Peter I like Clar because she is nice. My other friend Holly was in the car to. Holly and Clar got hurt.

Clar got a bump on her head and Holly got a bruise on her from the seetbelt.

them. The student in the example below combined drawing and writing. He recorded two problems involving ordering numbers and explained how to solve the first. His diagram (resembling a computer Windows screen) illustrates the meaning of "perimeter." On the same page he critiques a test.

The fifth-grade teachers use only dialogue journals. Students write for twenty minutes each day and are required to produce a minimum of six sentences and a picture in

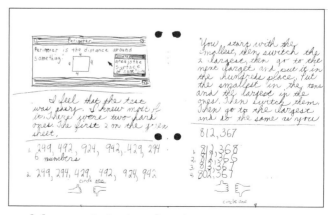

at least two colors. The date and day must start each entry. A list of these requirements is taped to each journal. It includes spaces within which the teachers check off the requirements that have been met each day. (This list has sufficient spaces for two weeks' entries.)

These teachers write a daily response to each student. This takes them approximately two hours each day, but they feel that the payoff of getting to know their students well is worth the time expended.

Teachers from many other schools have shared their ideas for using journals. The following are a few examples that illustrate the variety of possible applications. While we have included the grade level in which the lesson was first used, all these ideas can be adapted for older or younger children.

Unit on Spring–Grade 1

(ADRIENNE GILLET)

DAY 1

Close observation: Take a twenty- to thirty-minute walk around the schoolyard or a local park with the students to observe signs of spring using the senses of sight, sound, smell, and touch: for example, flowers (sight and smell), birds and bees (sight and sound), pussy willows (smell and touch). Ask the children to think about how spring makes them feel. Return to class and discuss the students' observations and how they felt. Then have the children record their observations in their journals. Extend the assignment by having students make the same kind of observations in their neighborhoods after school.

DAY 2

Discuss the signs of spring that the children observed in their neighborhoods. Have the children record these observations in their journals.

DAY 3

Webbing: Write *spring* in the center of the chalkboard. Then as you record them on the chalkboard and make the connections, have students brainstorm all the words and phrases they associate with spring. After this is finished, ask the children to write three things describing spring using the sentence starter "Spring is..."

DAY 4

Me-maps: Have children express their ideas and feelings about spring by illustrating what "Spring is..." (One girl wrote: "Spring is hearts floating down in the sky." Her picture was charming—various-sized hearts coming out of clouds and streaming to earth, where a little girl was reaching up to catch one.)

DAY 5

Listing: Using the topic Spring Things to Do, list on the chalkboard everything that comes to students' minds. Later, have children make their own lists in their journals.

DAY 6

Free writing: Have children write a story about spring. It can be about anything they wish and may be based on their feelings and observations taken from their previous journal entries.

DAY 7

Me-maps: Have children illustrate their stories using pictures.

DAY 8

On the final day, have group sharing of stories and illustrations. Let anyone who wishes read a story to the class.

Unit on Fruit Flies–Grade 2
(DIANE BAERWALD)

Observing the life cycle of the fruit fly is one unit in our district's science curriculum for second grade. A supply company provides the fruit flies, and my class spends weeks studying them. The flies are housed in little round plastic cases that rest (most of the time) on the corner of each student's desk.

Before beginning an in-depth study of the fruit flies, I open the unit with a discussion about the insects. During a brainstorming session, I record all the facts contributed by the children on a large sheet of paper titled "What We Know About Fruit Flies." The next day, on a second sheet, we list "Everything We Want to Know About Fruit Flies." A third sheet is reserved for "Everything We've Learned About Fruit Flies." Students fill that in as we study the insects.

As a class, we gather information from books, videos, movies, and other instructional materials. This gives us the background we need to make observations and predictions about the flies. During each science lesson I allow time for the children to read over the charts, make predictions, and enter new ideas about what they are learning.

Where do journals fit into this process? In addition to their personal journals, each child keeps a Science Learning Log. I make this as simple as possible because of the second-graders' limited writing skills. I tape a 5-by-7 in. (13-by-18 cm) card to each child's desk with his or her name and the date. I find the note cards easier for young children to begin with because the cards are small and easily accessible. On designated days we make observations, and they record them on their cards. They are free to add other interesting notes on other days if they wish. When a child fills a card, I save it in a folder and tape a new one to the desk.

The Science Learning Log entries vary from observable facts, such as the number of flies, to questions about what causes moisture in the cases. Because of space and time limitations, I respond to their logs verbally. This is easy since the cards are displayed all the time.

At the end of the experiment, the group completes the third large chart by filling in data from that already recorded in the learning logs. As a final project, the note cards are mounted on colored construction paper, illustrations are added, and cards are then bound into individual learning logs. The children proudly take these home to share with their parents.

Many children also write about fruit flies in their personal journals. There are creative stories, such as "The Giant Fruit Fly," and nonfiction accounts that expand the learning log entries. The children begin to feel like real scientists as they build concepts about insects, using actual processes such as observation and prediction.

Unit on Sioux Indians and Custer's Last Stand–Grade 5
(OPAL OSS)

Time period: two weeks

DAY 1

Webbing: Have students brainstorm ideas on customs and materials associated with Native Americans as you record and connect them on the chalkboard.

DAY 2

Learning logs: Have students respond to an article in paragraph or double-column form in their textbook about the Sioux and Custer's Last Stand, giving their reactions, asking questions, or recording their thoughts about the author's information.

DAY 3

Buddy journals: Ask students to write to their buddies about what they've studied throughout the unit.

DAY 4

Alternate point of view: Have students write about the war using one of the following topics: Major Reno's,

Captain Benteen's, Chief Sitting Bull's, or Crazy Horse's reaction to one of the events studied.

DAY 5

Buddy journals: Have students respond to their buddies' journals. (See Day 3.)

DAY 6

Learning logs: Have students record their reactions, questions, and thoughts to and about information in the textbook. If they used paragraph form the previous week, they now use the double-entry form or vice versa.

DAY 7

Buddy journals: Communications continue. (See Day 3.)

DAY 8

Unsent letters: Have students write a letter to President Ulysses S. Grant regarding the treatment of Indians and the takeover of aboriginal lands.

DAY 9

Buddy journals: Communications continue. (See Day 3.)

DAY 10

Have students list customs, people, places, materials, and events associated with the Sioux Indians and the battle now known as Custer's Last Stand.

Our Trip to the Zoo–Grade 2
(MARIE HOHNSTEIN)

My class will soon be taking a field trip to the zoo. This is the outline I use when beginning my annual unit on the zoo.

The first activity is a webbing activity, which takes place before our field trip. I dress up in a tiger suit and tell a fictional story about a trip I took to the zoo and all the creatures I saw there. This helps my students recall what they have seen on previous trips to the zoo. Then we do a web with the word *zoo* in the center.

On our field trip, while we're at the zoo together, we talk about the things the students see, hear, touch, smell, and feel. When we return to the classroom, we do a five senses poem (I see…I hear…I smell…I touch…I feel…), and then the students write lists in their journals of the creatures they saw.

The final activity involves altered point of view. The children each take the role of an animal they have observed and write about their life in the zoo. Later we all guess which animal each child has chosen.

The following are sample lessons from classroom teachers. We have included the grade levels of the teachers who shared these ideas, but the ideas they represent can easily be adapted to fit other grades.

Lesson on the Story of Chicken Little–Grade 2
(MARY MOORE)

Objectives

   After reading the story of Chicken Little and discussing the role of each character in the story, students will demonstrate the ability to (a) retell the story and (b) relate specifically to one character.

Introductory activity

   I introduce the story by asking riddles. For example: "I am a chicken. I thought the sky was falling. Who am I?"

   Students write their answers on little chalkboards and share them at my signal. I then ask a second riddle such as the following: "I wasn't liked very much. I tried to trick Chicken Little. Who am I?"

   Again students write their answers on the chalkboards. I tell the students that by now they have probably guessed they will be reading the story of Chicken Little.

Main activity

   I give each student a supply of little chicken cutouts. They write difficult words or phrases on them, then read these aloud. I read the story aloud while the students follow along. I introduce the journal-entry assignment by first modeling an entry and then explaining altered point of view. I set out pens and pencils. After students write their altered-point-of-view entry, they divide into small groups to share them aloud.

Evaluation

I evaluate the length and clarity of the entries. If the entries are not clear, I know my directions were unclear.

Lesson on Mental Clearing–Grade 4

(STACY WOOD)

Objective

Students will be able to express personal ideas, concerns, and emotions clearly through written expression.

Activity

I have students free-write without lifting pencil from paper for five to fifteen minutes.

Procedure

I explain to students that if something is taking up a lot of space in our brains, we can often help ourselves by getting it down on paper. Then we are able to concentrate on other things. I give some examples of things that could be on students' minds when they come to school in the morning: an argument with a family member, a social studies test, after-school plans. Then I explain that journals can be used as a place to store those thoughts. I read excerpts from my own journal to demonstrate that the journal can be a friend to talk to about concerns. I set the timer for the allotted time and ask my students to begin writing.

Lesson on Me-Map–Grade 4

(STACY WOOD)

Objectives

Students will be able to record and then sequence ten major events of their lives.

Activity

In at least two thirty-minute sessions students create me-maps.

Procedure

Have students discuss the major events that have occurred in their lives and then ask them to record at least ten such events in their journals. Ask how these events could be communicated using some method other than written or spoken words. Display an incomplete me-map and share with students the meaning of some of the symbols. Ask students to add some events. Then ask them to construct a rough draft of a me-map in their journals. These will later be transferred to large paper and displayed in the room.

WHAM Lesson–Grade 6
(LESLIE OSBORNE)

Objective

The student will write a list of thoughts, feelings, or words that come to mind about a specific topic.

Introduction

I ask the children to think of some of the things we use lists for, such as grocery items, things to do, letters to Santa. (Listing is one of the journaling techniques.) I explain that lists of words can be made for lots and lots of topics, such as music groups. Then I ask them to help me make a short list of music groups, then pets, then TV shows.

Activity

After they've practiced with these lists, I explain that they are going to be making lists in their journals. "I'll tell you the topic and how many minutes you have. Then you write down at least ten—twenty is better—things on your list. Don't worry about getting things in the right order and don't worry about spelling. Keep working on the list until the time is up."

I then ask them to write one of my favorite lists—a WHAM (What's Hot About Me) list. First I list things about me for about one minute. I then ask them to write WHAM at the top of one of their journal pages and then list "some of the things that are hot about you." I give them five minutes and ask them to keep writing until the time is up.

Outline for an Eight-Week Journaling Program–Grade 4
(CHARLYNNE HERMANN)

WEEK 1

MONDAY

Students discuss journaling and get their notebooks ready.

WEDNESDAY

Students complete artwork for the covers of their journals.

FRIDAY

The teacher demonstrates me-maps and has students practice making them.

WEEK 2

MONDAY

Students discuss and make their own me-maps in their journals.

WEDNESDAY

The teacher demonstrates webbing and has students practice this technique.

FRIDAY

Students write at least three sentences on Wednesday's webbing topic. The teacher reviews students' journals.

WEEK 3

MONDAY

Students discuss progress on their journals and then brainstorm topics that could be used for free writing. The teacher demonstrates free writing and has students practice this technique.

WEDNESDAY

Students free-write on the topic My Family.

FRIDAY

Students free-write on the topic Do You Like Journaling?

WEEK 4

MONDAY

Students do maps or webbing on the topic of pets.

WEDNESDAY

Students free-write for five to ten minutes on the topic The Pet I'd Like to Have.

FRIDAY

Students free-write for five to ten minutes on the topic Important Things to Remember About Pets. The teacher reviews students' journals.

WEEK 5

MONDAY

Students free-write on topics from their own lists (see Week 3) and discuss the different ideas chosen. Those who wish share their work with the class.

WEDNESDAY

Students free-write using prompts such as "Once upon a time…" or "There once was a…"

FRIDAY

Students can choose to free-write or create webs or me-maps. The teacher reviews students' journals and writes a comment and a question in each child's journal as an introduction to dialogue journals.

WEEK 6

MONDAY

The teacher explains dialogue journals: "It's a lot like playing catch. If you throw the ball and your partner doesn't return it, then there's no game. To dialogue you must make a comment or ask a question. The other person must react to it without using yes or no in order to keep the conversation going." Role-play this or ask students to try it with a partner.

WEDNESDAY

Students free-write using the topic lists in their journals.

FRIDAY

Students choose to free-write or create webs or me-maps.

WEEK 7

MONDAY AND WEDNESDAY

Students free-write, knowing that the teacher will respond to their work once a week.

FRIDAY

Students choose to free-write or create webs or me-maps.

WEEK 8

MONDAY AND WEDNESDAY

Students free-write, knowing that the teacher will respond to their work once a week.

FRIDAY

Students choose to free-write or create webs or me-maps.

ONGOING JOURNALING ACTIVITIES

The following are suggestions from teachers for ongoing journaling activities using learning logs, buddy journals, and "weekend windows."

Learning Logs

(SYLVIA STARR)

Objective

> Students reflect on a lesson just completed to create a record for future review.

Activity

> Students write in their journals after all hands-on science lessons. (This could be expanded to other content-area lessons.)

Procedure

> I write student-generated responses on the board, reviewing what happened during the lesson. Students draw a line down the middle of a page in their spiral notebooks. On the left side of the page, they copy the review from the board. On the right side, they write their comments, opinions, questions, or previous experiences related to the subject dealt with in the lesson.

Evaluation

> The journals are not graded. However, every child is expected to keep one. I write a response in each child's journal every week.

Buddy Journals Between Classrooms–Grade 3

(CAMI ADKISSON AND JONI FLORY)

CAMI: Joni and I wanted to have our classes do buddy journals. I really enjoyed doing this type of journal in class and thought my students would like it too. We made two sets of spiral-bound journals, one with pink covers and one with blue. We assigned each student a number, so we ended up with Pink-1, Pink-2, and so on and matched them with Blue-1, Blue-2, and so on. The students could decorate their journals in any way they wanted, but they had to use the number in the decoration.

The students really liked the idea of not knowing who their buddies were. Joni and I decided to give them a "starter" idea to begin their writing to their unknown journal buddies. We had them write about their favorite weekend activities. They could elaborate as much as they wanted and also write about anything else that came to mind.

JONI: At first we had the kids writing to "secret" buddies, but it didn't take them long to figure out who their buddies were. In fact, writing questions to help them identify their mystery writing partners kept the pencils flying across the paper quite well for a while. Now the students in my class switch journals with their buddies in Cami's class twice weekly and look forward to this.

CAMI: I've increased the amount of time I give the students to write in their journals from five to ten minutes. They really like this communication time with another peer. One problem I've noticed is that students get a little offended when their partners don't write as much as they do. I have suggested they ask their partners to tell more about themselves.

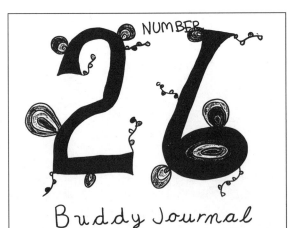

JONI: We'll continue buddy journals for as long as the kids want. They're already asking if they can change secret buddies next month.

Weekend Windows–Grade 2

(SHARON LEITHAUSER)

"Weekend windows" combine the techniques of me-maps and free writing. They draw on students' interest in illustration and their positive experience with free writing. They are an ongoing activity, which students tell me are "the funnest thing we do."

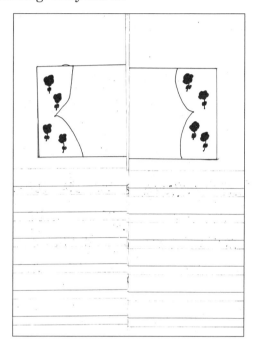

On Monday morning after roll call, I give each student a large (12-by-22 inch or 30-by-55 cm) sheet of paper. I instruct the students to fold the paper down the center, lay it flat on their desks, then fold both the left and right sides of the paper to the center.

The students then draw a window on the two folded halves (right). They color in curtains, windowpanes, the horizon, or whatever else they want. Once they have finished the window, they open the sheet of paper and use the bottom half of the paper to write about something that happened during the weekend. They illustrate the event on the top half (below).

There are always a number who volunteer to show their pictures and read their weekend-window story to the class. Later I pass around the three-hole punch, have the students punch the left side of their "windows," and then put brads in the holes.

I repeat the process every week, so at the end of the term they have a book of weekend windows.

An alternative is "Friday doors." In this version students fold sheets of paper in half and draw a door on the outside. They open their doors and write about their plans for the weekend. As with weekend windows, students illustrate their stories.

7

This chapter includes a list of the questions about journaling most frequently asked by teachers and our responses to these questions.

Help! This is too much work! I'm taking home stacks of journals each night. How can I manage this?

If teachers commit to reading every entry in every student's journal every week, most soon discover that the paper load is far too great. The following are some management ideas that have worked well for teachers:

- Ask students to star one or two entries per week for you to read.

- Collect journals from only part of the class each day—a row, table, or group.

- Move around the room as students write and respond on the spot, verbally or in writing.

- Use adult volunteers or older students to read journals and write comments in them.

Kids often tell me more than I really want to know about their personal lives, but how can I ignore them when they ask for advice?

Occasionally, students write pages and pages about troubles they are experiencing at school or home, and teachers find themselves placed in a counseling role. Be careful not to fall into the trap of thinking you have to try to solve all their problems. Use other professional resource persons and refer major issues to counselors.

Nothing says you must structure your journal assignments to encourage personal revelations. If you are uncomfortable hearing too much about sensitive issues, then use learning logs or assigned topics that leave little room for digression. Each of us has our own comfort level in this and all other areas of teaching.

How do I respond to other teachers or parents who feel that journal writing is a frivolous activity?

Unfortunately, some teachers and students have had negative experiences with journaling and regard it as a "soft" process, one that is, at best, a time filler and, at worst, a time waster. Many people equate classroom journals to daily diary keeping; others have never kept a journal themselves. These critics have a limited perspective about the kinds of journals and techniques that can be used and their wide range of applications across the curriculum.

Use your mission statement to explain your rationale and show colleagues the range of journaling applications. Remember that criticism affords an opportunity for dialogue. If your main goal with journaling is to get to know your students better, give an example of how that knowledge has helped you reach a difficult student. If you use journals in math or social studies, demonstrate how you've integrated journaling into the curriculum. If your mission statement has been grounded in educational objectives, you are well prepared to respond to criticism.

How can I get my students to take journals seriously?

Journals become little more than an empty exercise if you don't have clear educational objectives. Keeping the class busy while you take attendance is not an educational objective. When assigned for this kind of purpose, students will regard journaling as busy work and cease to respond seriously. By the same token, if you don't take journals seriously, they will become the first thing to go if timing is tight. Start small, be sure to keep your learning objectives clearly in mind, and design a schedule that fits easily into your current curriculum.

I've tried journals, and they've never worked. Why should I try them again?

You may feel frustrated for one of several reasons. If journals are collected and then not returned for a long time, students quickly lose interest. Another reason teachers become discouraged and students become bored is because teachers often rely on only one journaling technique. In this book we suggest a comprehensive approach that encourages choosing from several types and techniques of journaling. The many forms of entries will appeal to students with different learning preferences and aptitudes as well as to different grade levels.

What do I say to parents who will not permit their child's participation in journal writing because they believe that "school is no place to teach family values"?

Meet with the parents to learn more about their objections. Answer any questions they might have and show them your guidelines. Invite them to suggest journaling topics. Offer all students in your class the choice of at least two topics. If that still does not satisfy the parents, allow the child a free choice of topic. The only rule for that child is that he or she must write or draw *something* during journaling time.

How can journal writing improve writing skills if I let students make the same mistakes over and over again?

Our experience has been that, as students mature, they tend to conform more and more to conventions of standard English. Therefore, while we promote journal writing with little emphasis on mechanics, we also advocate direct instruction on specific skills. Many teachers use the mistakes they see repeated in students' journals as springboards for mini-lessons. For example, if a large number of students are combining plural subjects with singular verb forms (or vice versa), you may seize the opportunity to teach a lesson on subject–verb agreement.

The revising and editing steps of the writing process are where the work of correcting writing errors is done. One of the most effective ways of using journals to improve skills is to have students regularly choose entries to edit for a grade, for sharing, or for publication.

Dialogue journals provide teachers with excellent opportunities to help individual students improve their skills. When you *show* students correct spelling and punctuation rather than putting red pen slashes on all their errors, they strive to emulate your writing rather than dwell on what they did wrong. (Please be sure that your own spelling and punctuation are correct. Unfortunately, we have seen many errors made by teachers in dialogue journals.)

Isn't it bad to let students use invented, or creative, spelling?

While we do urge you to let students use "guess-and-go" spelling in their journals (and in their early drafts of writing), this does not mean that we feel that correct spelling is unimportant. If you insist that students spell correctly in their journals, their work will be limited to what they can spell.

This usually results in shallow stories, because the children may lack the spelling vocabulary to express complex thoughts (Calkins 1986; Hansen 1985; Routman 1993). Invented spelling is part of a developmental process, and most children move out of that stage and advance toward more sophisticated methods of attacking spelling (Fulwiler 1987; Moffett and Wagner 1993; Routman 1993; Strickland 1990).

To help children with their spelling, we suggest taking class spelling words from the children's writing. Use the words the children attempt to spell as they explain a current topic and those that are consistently misspelled as the basis for your spelling lessons.

I don't like webbing. Why should I teach this technique?

Different journaling techniques appeal to different types of learners. Some students in the class probably won't warm to webbing either, but some will love it. After you've taught the concept, be honest with your students about webbing not being your favorite technique. But at the same time acknowledge that it works wonderfully well for some writers.

I don't have the time to write in my journal at the same time as my students. Is this really important?

While we do think this is important, we know it is not always possible. Write when you can, even if it's not during class time, and occasionally read one of your journal entries aloud. If students know you are keeping a journal too, that is almost as powerful an influence as your writing with them every day.

How can I maintain discipline if I am writing in my journal while they do?

Some teachers are concerned that if their attention is on their journal writing for ten or fifteen minutes, students will become unruly. If you don't feel comfortable writing while your students write, try one of the following approaches:

 ✐ Write your journal entries outside of class and bring them in to share with students.

 ✐ See that students are settled at work on their journals, write for one or two minutes, then check on them again before writing a few more lines.

 ✐ Encourage volunteers or aides to keep journals and write when the students do.

What if students won't write in their journals?

Ask questions. Find out if they are uncomfortable with any part of the guidelines. Clarify the issues of confidentiality and purpose. Many times this bridges the gap. The following are some other ideas:

- If students say "I don't know what to write," ask them to write that sentence in their journals. Some repetitions of that phrase may lead to their writing about their feelings and speculating about what they would rather be doing.

- Give students the option of using a technique different from the one suggested or of drawing.

- Ask students to describe what they see around them.

- Keep a file of pictures that may prompt ideas for writing.

You may find that some students who frequently object to assignments or act out will use journaling to express ideas, feelings, and attitudes that surprise or enlighten you.

Can I use journals with my ESL students?

Yes. Dialogue journals are especially effective with ESL students. However, this is the one exception to the admonition not to mark errors in students' writing. Many ESL students prefer to have all their errors noted because they are highly motivated to write "correct" English.

Can I use journals with kindergarten students?

Journals are an ideal place for children in kindergarten to explore the correlation of letters, sounds, and objects. The process of recording letters and words reinforces children's positive experiences with language. Drawing in their journals and then dictating thoughts to a teacher or aide who prints these in their journals works well for kindergarten students.

8

MAKING CONNECTIONS

If we could decree how children are to be taught, we would have teachers follow these directives: Give writing the same priority as reading and math. Use a whole-language approach in which journals are fully integrated into instruction throughout the day. Journals are natural adjuncts to the writing process, to writer's workshop, to whole-language learning, and to informal assessment.

THE WRITING PROCESS

We think of journaling as a natural tool for writing instruction, and indeed that is one of its greatest values. People of all ages use journals as writers' notebooks—ideal for brainstorming and first drafts.

Writing is a process that has several steps. The first step is prewriting or exploring, in which journals can play a logical role. Journal entries include a wealth of unedited impressions and images. Some are the equivalent of doodling, meaningless notes that will go no further; others contain the germs of good writing ideas.

In the second step of the writing process, those unformed ideas are organized into a rough draft; a first attempt at creating a story, reminiscence, report, letter, or poem. Students use their journals to find a topic to write about. They go through their entries until they come across something that they want to spend time on. Then they create a "sloppy copy" on that topic. It's important that students write first drafts quickly and not try to write, revise, and edit at the same time. The style is similar to that of free focused writing, with the focus on content.

Many writers use their prewriting, especially their webs and lists, to plan their first drafts. Instead of using an outline, which is too linear and detailed for some learners, students number ideas on their webs or color-code items on their lists as a way of organizing their material.

Once a first draft is complete, the student can review it to see what revision is required, often reading the draft aloud or showing it to a classmate for feedback. At this stage writers are trying to read with new eyes to see if their purposes are being met. This may generate several more drafts as portions are added or deleted, shifted to new locations, or reworded. Only after this part of the process is finished does the emphasis shift to mechanics. For young children, the revision may be limited to adding a few words or another sentence. Even if the changes are slight, the idea of what revision means will get across.

After the revision stage is complete, students bring a critical eye to the writing and catch errors of spelling, punctuation, and usage. They may show copies to trusted classmates for their feedback. Many teachers use checklists for peer editors to mark as they check other writers' work.

Finally, the process is complete when the writing is published: made public by being printed and bound in a book, read aloud to attentive classmates, or posted on an author's board.

This, in a nutshell, is the writing process, a creative act about which much has been written. Journals fit logically into this scheme for the beginning steps of prewriting and drafting. In many classrooms journals are used primarily as writers' notebooks in which each entry is a potential story, poem, or other work. Students create journal entries with the expectation that they will be asked to develop and refine some of them for publishing.

Some teachers ask that students choose one journal entry a week and polish it before sharing it with a class or a buddy. Writing for an audience motivates the children—and us—to make revisions. Indeed, why do we revise any piece of writing if not to make our meaning clear for others? If students know others will be privy to their writing, it inspires them to complete the writing process.

A key strategy...is to put students in a position of writing from plenty rather than from scarcity. Instead of facing blank paper and a bare topic and having to strain for something to say, the students start off with a problem of selecting out—composing or abstracting—that is easier to deal with and educationally more to the point. (Moffett 1992)

The Writing Process

Prewrite / Explore

Think about all the ideas on a topic. Put them on paper any way you like: webbing, listing, free writing, or drawing. Remember to write any idea that comes to mind.

Write the First Draft

Look at your prewriting ideas and decide which ones to include in your first draft. Mark them with numbers, stars, or colors to help you decide what order to put them in. Write the first draft as fast as you can. This is a sloppy copy, so don't worry about spelling and punctuation.

Revise and Rewrite

Read the first draft. See if it says what you want it to. If it doesn't, make any changes it needs. You might add more sentences, move some sentences, add or erase some words. Then show it to another student. Get more opinions on what you might add or change.

Edit and Write Final Draft

Wait a day, then check your writing for mistakes. Correct spelling, capitalization, grammar, and punctuation. Ask another student to edit your writing. When you are sure it is as good as you can get it, write a final copy.

Publish

Writing is meant to be read. You have choices on how to publish your writing: make a book, post it on a wall, read it from the author's chair.

WRITER'S WORKSHOP

Writer's workshop, as we refer to it, is a structured situation in which students share drafts at all stages of the writing process—from prewriting through any number of revisions and edits. With each new version of the text, the writers solicit responses from peers (and adults). The writing process does not demand that students participate in writer's workshop; however, many teachers have discovered peer review to be a highly effective way of engaging students in revising and editing.

For example, Ramon has created a web in his journal about his family's first trip to the zoo over the weekend. He would like to write an account of this adventure, but doesn't know how to get started. He shows his three tablemates his web drawn in colored pens and asks for their help. In turn, they question him:

- "Was it like you thought it would be?"
- "What did you see first?"
- "What did you like the best?"

Ramon stops them. "That's it! I'll start with what I liked the best."

It's all over in less than five minutes, and they return to their independent work. Ramon doesn't always follow his classmates' advice, but in this case they have helped him overcome writer's block. He continues to ask for their comments and ideas as he writes, revises, and edits.

The writer's workshop approach, incorporating the writing process, gives maximum independence to student writers. Working from their journal entries, they develop the pieces that interest them the most, using their class-mates as resource people. This frees the teacher to hold writing conferences with individual students. At other times, the teacher groups students who are stumped by a similar writing problem and conducts a mini-lesson on that subject.

Children are eager to read their peers' writing and to hear encouraging reactions or helpful suggestions about their own work. Reading each other's writing creates an

even stronger and more personal reading-writing connection
than does responding to professional authors' work.

> Reading and writing...are considered integrated processes.
> Writing generates an enthusiasm for reading, and reading
> creates the impetus for writing. As children write stories, they
> organize their thoughts onto paper and analyze them during
> peer conferences. During class sharing and response time,
> children listen for contextual meaning in stories written by
> their peers. (Robbins 1990)

Of course, this does not happen overnight. Just as teachers
must teach journaling techniques and each step of the
writing process, they must also teach children how to hold
writers' conferences with their peers.

WHOLE-LANGUAGE LEARNING

Journal writing and the writer's workshop fit seamlessly
into the whole-language classroom where children are
immersed in speaking, listening, reading, and writing
experiences.

In a typical whole-language classroom

> ...the language arts are used, not "covered." Writing and
> speaking, as well as reading and listening, are exploited as
> the natural means by which these fifth-graders learn history,
> biography, astronomy, physics, economics, politics, geography,
> and literature. The written and spoken word flourishes in this
> class because they are *not* separated from the rest of the
> curriculum for "special attention," but are allowed to be used
> for their best purposes: problem solving, group communications,
> and performance. (Jeffries-Thaiss and Thaiss 1984)

Teachers who use the whole-language approach facilitate
discovery rather than dispense knowledge. Their classrooms are student-centered with less teacher talk and a
corresponding increase in student talk. By providing
students with more choices and giving them opportunities

to learn from their mistakes, the responsibility for learning is shifted to the student. Teachers remain the informed, conscientious adults whose task it is to guide and focus their young charges on their journeys.

Whole-language teachers have put aside their basal readers and skill-based workbooks in favor of a functional approach in which language skills are used throughout the day. Their instructional plans resemble the natural language learning that children experience in daily life. Children repeatedly see logos on television, learn what familiar neighborhood signs mean, and note that their mothers write to-do lists, which are posted on the refrigerator. With this thought in mind, the journal becomes an accessory available throughout the day.

For example, Emile, a fifth-grader, first drafts a letter in his journal to his Greek pen pal, then makes a web about a filmstrip on the respiratory system, and, filling in an idle moment, sketches an idea for a skateboard design that occurred to him while reading a magazine article. During the last five minutes before the bell rings, Emile summarizes his feelings about the school day. In this way, each day's odyssey of education takes shape through language.

> In these [whole-language] classrooms, students' uses of reading and writing are inseparable, and children's in-school uses of literacy are wholly consistent with the reading and writing experiences that occur in their daily lives. Neither students nor teachers are distracted by clocks and textbooks which signal spelling time, handwriting time, English time, reading time, and writing time. (Jensen and Roser 1990)

Students in such classrooms, trusty journals at their sides, use all kinds of language skills as an integral part of each day's instruction. They speak, listen, write, and read as they, for example, work through a thematic unit on the ocean. This unit might incorporate the following journaling requirements:

- Read and write poems about sea creatures.
- Research and discuss tsunamis.

✐ Write letters to oceanographers, then read any replies received.

✐ Listen to the recorded sounds of whales calling across ocean depths and respond by drawing.

INFORMAL ASSESSMENT

Journals can be used to assess a class's knowledge prior to a subject being taught or to follow an individual student's progress. In both cases, they help instructors assess students' knowledge.

Bob Runningbear's class is scheduled to study geology, so he decides to lead them in a class web to assess what they know already. He first asks his sixth-graders to open their journals to a fresh page and write the word *geology* in preparation for a list or web. He allows the class five minutes to record information and questions about the subject. He encourages them to brainstorm about their knowledge or experiences with geology.

Bob then writes the word *geology* in the center of the chalkboard and asks students to share some of the items from their journals. Francesca says, "Geology's the study of rocks." Jeremiah adds, "Mountains, too." As students contribute to the class web, Bob records their contributions on the board and gets a good idea of their knowledge and attitudes about geology. He realizes that some students confuse geology and geography, while most of the class understands that mountains and rocks are part of what they will be studying. This process also introduces the unit to the students through their own participation.

As Bob plans his curriculum, he takes into account the class's previous knowledge. He asks students to use their journals throughout the unit, including keeping learning logs on the weather and writing about a volcano from an altered point of view.

Bob chose to do a class web at the end of the geology unit. This time he guided the webbing by creating the categories of plate tectonics, magnetic poles, and potential energy sources from the oceans. As a result, he was able to informally assess what students had learned.

Journals also provide a respectful, positive way to analyze and correct students' errors in grammar, punctuation, and spelling. This is particularly true of dialogue journals. As each student builds an ongoing written conversation with the teacher, specific skill weaknesses become clear. One of the desired outcomes in Angelica Escame's third-grade class is that students write in complete sentences. As she reads her student's journals, she watches for repeated structure errors.

In October Krystal writes: "Over the weekend. Me and my mom bot too cakes. One for me and one for my sister to."

Angelica notes that Krystal continues to write in fragments and is confusing the homonym's *too*, *to*, and *two*. She responds in dialogue journal format: "I went to the store over the weekend too. I bought two new dresses. One dress is red. One is blue. My favorite dress is the red one. What color is your favorite dress?"

The following week, Krystal writes back: "My red dress is my favorite dress two. I saw your red dress on munday."

Angelica Escame continues the dialogue by choosing words and phrases that correct Krystal's mistakes through example. Thus the journal acts as an agent to show Krystal's errors and as a tool for remediation.

Angelica's next entry reads: "Yes, Krystal. I did wear my red dress on Monday. I will wear my blue dress this week, too. I will wear it on Friday."

Krystal responds by writing: "I will wear my blue dress on friday, too. I will wear my red dress on monday."

Over time, Krystal's sentences and her use of homonyms and capital letters become more consistently correct. Angelica has taught by example and given more attention to the things that Krystal does right than to those she does wrong. In this way the teacher can do specific prescriptive remediation that responds to student needs. As a result, each student is able to progress at his or her own pace.

Journal entries allow a comprehensive view of a child's skill development and thinking processes. They can give clues to visual or auditory dyslexia and spelling pattern errors. Because the flow of words, ideas, and images is spontaneous, errors occur naturally. A teacher may notice that a second-grader consistently confuses lowercase forms of d, b, p, and q. She may then consult with the special education or resource room teacher about remediation techniques. Once the teacher learns that this is typical of auditory dyslexia and that kinesthetic and auditory practice and repetition can help, she can help the child in that specific area.

IN CONCLUSION

Journal writing is a lifelong skill. Many people who started keeping journals in childhood cherish these chronicles of their lives. Denise Abbey, 84, started a diary in childhood at the insistence of her father—not a teacher. Although she has never been published, she has written extensively throughout her life and continues to write daily. Denise shared these thoughts about journaling:

> When I was twelve years old, my father gave me a five-year diary and said, "Doll, I'd like you to keep this."

> So I began, and I kept at it until it was filled. By then, I was accustomed to writing every day, so I asked Dad for another volume, which he gladly gave me. That almost covered my college years, and the third one dealt with my graduation and first years working in the mountains of North Carolina. By that time, try as I would to condense my writing, I needed more space. So I bought a large one-year journal. Finally, even these were too small, and I graduated to book size, and now I have more than thirty of them. They cover my life, with a few exceptions: a time when one was lost in a hotel fire; a period after my baggage was stolen; and the year 1944 and part of 1945 during my service overseas when I was forbidden to keep a diary.

Your students have much to gain from their journals. They will have a record of their days, one that, like Denise Abbey's, may eventually span a lifetime. Journal writing will provide them with quiet time in which to ponder the mysteries of their lives, from the confusion of learning fractions to the dilemma of divorcing parents. It will give them a place and opportunity to make mistakes, to rehearse their responses to questions without fear of exposing their vulnerability.

We invite you to join your students by keeping your own personal or classroom journal. Opening to a blank journal page is the first step on an exciting journey.

Aulls, Mark W. "Understanding the Relationship Between Reading and Writing." *Educational Horizons* 64 (1) (1985): 39–44.

Barbe, Walter B., and Raymond H. Swassing. *Teaching Through Modality Strengths: Concepts and Practices*. Columbus, OH: Zaner-Bloser, 1979.

Blackburn, Ellen. "Common Ground: Developing Relationships Between Reading and Writing." *Language Arts* 61 (4) (1984): 367–75.

Bloom, Benjamin. *Taxonomy of Educational Objectives: The Classification of Educational Goals, by a Committee of College and University Examiners*. 1st ed. New York: Longmans, Green, 1956–66.

Bode, Barbara A. "Dialogue Journal Writing." *The Reading Teacher* 42 (8) (April 1989): 568–71.

Butler, Kathleen. *Learning and Teaching Style in Theory and Practice*. Columbia, CT: The Learner's Dimension, 1988.

Calkins, Lucy McCormick. *The Art of Teaching Writing*. Portsmouth, NH: Heinemann, 1986.

Countryman, Joan. *Writing to Learn Mathematics*. Portsmouth, NH: Heinemann, 1992.

Farr, Marcia. "Writing Growth in Young Children: What We Are Learning from Research." In *Speaking and Writing, K–12*, edited by Christopher Thaiss and Charles Suhor, pp. 125–43. Urbana, IL: National Council of Teachers of English, 1984.

Fulwiler, Toby. "The Politics of Writing Across the Curriculum." Paper presented at the National Council of Teachers of English Commission on Composition, November 22, 1986. ERIC Document Reproduction Service, no. ED 276 601.

——. "Writing and Learning in Grade Three." In *The Journal Book*, edited by Toby Fulwiler, pp. 193–97. Portsmouth, NH: Heinemann, 1987.

Gardner, Howard. *Frames of Mind: The Theory of Multiple Intelligences*. New York: Basic Books, 1983.

Geddes, LaDonna McMurray. "Journals as Part of the Learning Process." Paper presented at the 78th Annual Meeting of the Speech Communication Association, October 1992, at Chicago, Illinois. ERIC Document Reproduction Service, no. ED 354 520.

Guild, Pat, and Stephen Garger. *Marching to Different Drummers*. Alexandria, VA: Association for Supervision and Curriculum Development, 1988.

Hansen, Jane. "Skills." In *Breaking Ground: Teachers Relate Reading and Writing in the Elementary School*, edited by Jane Hansen, Thomas Newkirk, and Donald Graves, pp. 183–91. Portsmouth, NH: Heinemann, 1985.

Jeffries-Thaiss, Ann, and Christopher Thaiss. "Learning Better, Learning More: In the Home and Across the Curriculum." In *Speaking and Writing, K–12*, edited by Christopher Thaiss and Charles Suhor, pp. 1–28. Urbana, IL: National Council of Teachers of English, 1984.

Jensen, Julie M., and Nancy L. Roser. "Are There Really 3 R's?" *Educational Leadership* 47 (6) (March 1990): 7–12.

Kellogg, Steven, ed. *Chicken Little*. New York: William Morrow, 1941.

Kintisch, Lenore S. "Journal Writing: Stages of Development." *The Reading Teacher* 40 (2) (November 1986): 68–72.

Langer, Judith A., and Arthur N. Applebee. "Learning to Write: Learning to Think." *Educational Horizons* 64 (1) (Fall 1985): 36–38.

Lopez, Eileen B. "Dialogue Journal Writing in Kindergarten and First Grade Classrooms." Practicum paper, Nova University, 1990. ERIC Document Reproduction Service, no. ED 324 115.

Moffett, James. *Active Voice: A Writing Program Across the Curriculum*. 2nd ed. Portsmouth, NH: Heinemann, 1992.

Moffet, James, and Betty Jane Wagner. "What Works Is Play." *Language Arts* 70 (1) (January 1993): 32–36.

Raths, Louis E.; Selma Wasserman; Jonas Arthur; and Arnold Rothstein. *Teaching for Thinking: Theory, Strategies, and Activities for the Classroom*. 2nd ed. New York: Teachers College Press, 1986.

Robbins, Patricia A. "Implementing Whole Language: Bridging Children and Books." *Educational Leadership* 47 (6) (March 1990): 50–54.

Routman, Regie. "The Uses and Abuses of Invented Spelling." *Instructor* 102 (9) (May/June 1993): 36–39.

Sandmark, Laura, and George E. Coon. "Learning to Read by Writing About Reading." *Teaching K–8* 18 (6) (March 1988): 60–65.

Scieszka, Jon. *The True Story of the Three Little Pigs!* New York: Viking, 1989.

Shanahan, Timothy. "The Reading-Writing Relationship: Seven Instructional Principles." *The Reading Teacher* 41 (7) (March 1988): 636–47.

Staton, Jana. "The Power of Responding in Dialogue Journals." In *The Journal Book*, edited by Toby Fulwiler, pp. 47–53. Portsmouth, NH: Heinemann, 1987.

Stock, Gregory. *The Kids' Book of Questions*. New York: Workman, 1988.

Strickland, Dorothy S. "Emergent Literacy: How Young Children Learn to Read and Write." *Educational Leadership* 47 (6) (March 1990): 18–23.

Sullivan, Anne McCrary. "Liberating the Urge to Write: From Classroom Journals to Lifelong Writing." *English Journal* 78 (7) (November 1989): 55–61.

Tiedt, Iris McClellan, and National Writing Project Teacher Consultants (Ruth Gibbs, Martha Howard, Marylue Timpson, and Mary Young Williams). *Reading / Thinking / Writing: A Holistic Language and Literacy Program for the K–8 Classroom*. Boston: Allyn and Bacon, 1989.

Tierney, Robert J. "Redefining Reading Comprehension." *Educational Leadership* 47 (6) (March 1990): 37–42.

Tierney, Robert J.; Rebekah Caplan; Linnea Ehri; Mary Healy; and Mary Hurdlow. "Writing and Reading Working Together." In *Collaboration Through Writing and Reading*, edited by Anne Haas Dyson, pp. 169–209. Urbana, IL: National Council of Teachers of English, 1989.

Tompkins, Gail E. *Teaching Writing: Balancing Process and Product*. Columbus, OH: Merrill, 1990.

Wadlington, Elizabeth; Joe Bitner; Elizabeth Partridge; and Sue Austin. "Have a Problem? Make the Writing–Mathematics Connection!" *Arithmetic Teacher* 40 (4) (1992): 207–09.

Zacharis, Martha. "The Relationship Between Journal Writing in Education and Thinking Processes: What Educators Say About It." Self-published, 1990. ERIC Document Reproduction Service, no. ED 327 870.

The following are books and articles that have helped many teachers gain greater understanding of journaling. This list of recommended reading is divided into three sections: journaling for children, writing development and the writing process, books to read to children.

JOURNALING FOR CHILDREN

Bode, Barbara A. "Dialogue Journal Writing." *The Reading Teacher* 42 (8) (April 1989): 568–71.

Answers most questions about dialogue journals. Cites numerous studies that support the advantages of this form of journaling.

Bromley, Karen D'Angelo. "Buddy Journals Make the Reading–Writing Connection." *The Reading Teacher* 43 (2) (November 1989): 122–29.

Establishes that the rationale for using buddy journals is improvement in both reading and writing skills. Illustrated with examples of students' buddy journals.

Capacchione, Lucia. *The Creative Journal for Children*. Boston: Shambhala, 1989.

Seventy-two exercises in writing and drawing to foster children's creativity, self-esteem, and learning skills. Great prompts for getting started.

Dahlstrom, Lorraine M. *Writing Down the Days: 365 Creative Journaling Ideas for Young People*. Minneapolis: Free Spirit, 1990.

A journaling prompt for each day of the year. Includes historical, literary, and humorous allusions. Practical and motivating for more mature students.

Fulwiler, Toby, ed. *The Journal Book*. Portsmouth, NH: Boynton Cook, 1987.

Forty-two articles about journaling. Includes stories of teachers applying journals across the curriculum. Good range of grade levels and insights.

Heath, Gail. "Journals in a Classroom: One Teacher's Trials and Errors." *English Journal* 77(2) (February 1988): 58–60.

Learn from another teacher's mistakes! Explains how Heath adjusted her journal writing plan over a three-year period.

Kintisch, Lenore S. "Journal Writing: Stages of Development." *The Reading Teacher* 40 (2) (November 1986): 68–72.

Reports on a four-year study of journal writing in an elementary school. Describes patterns observed in each grade from kindergarten to grade four.

Kipfer, Barbara Ann. *14,000 Things to Be Happy About*. New York: Workmen, 1990.

Slightly silly list of 14,000 things that the author began writing at age twelve. Good example of a long, long list.

Parsons, Les. *Response Journals*. Portsmouth, NH: Heinemann, 1990.

Step-by-step system for incorporating reading and writing using responses to literature. Although written for secondary students, many ideas can be adapted for the intermediate grades. Includes lists of questions, criteria for evaluation, and record sheets.

Stock, Gregory. *The Kids' Book of Questions*. New York: Workman, 1988.

Two hundred and sixty questions that make it "easy to ask hard questions." Includes a range of topics about growing up, fantasy, self-esteem, relationships, and some silly stuff.

WRITING DEVELOPMENT AND THE WRITING PROCESS

Calkins, Lucy McCormick. *The Art of Teaching Writing*. Portsmouth, NH: Heinemann, 1986.

Knowledgeable work on how children develop as writers from kindergarten through adolescence. Extensive discussion of the writing process and writing conferences.

Evans, Joy, and Jo Ellen Moore. *How to Make Books with Children*. Monterey, CA: Evan-Moore, 1991.

Specific techniques on creating and binding books. Useful for adults and children who wish to turn journal entries into a more polished form.

Goldberg, Natalie. *Writing Down the Bones*. Boston: Shambhala, 1986.

A guide to timed-writing practice inspired by the principles of Zen. Includes lots of practical exercises nearly guaranteed to break writer's block.

Hansen, Jane; Thomas Newkirk; and Donald Graves; eds. *Breaking Ground: Teachers Relate Reading and Writing in the Elementary School*, Portsmouth, NH: Heinemann, 1985.

A collection of first-person experiences from a number of elementary teachers. Good discussions of invented spelling, reading-writing connections, and skill development.

Klauser, Henriette. *Writing on Both Sides of the Brain*. San Francisco: Harper and Row, 1987.

Upbeat writer's guide that advocates balancing the analytical left brain with the creative right brain. Clear, fun-filled guide through the writing process.

Moffett, James. *Active Voice: A Writing Program Across the Curriculum*. 2nd ed. Portsmouth, NH: Heinemann, 1992.

Detailed discussion of the writing process. Describes numerous writing activities for intermediate students that can be adapted to journal writing.

Rainier, Tristine. *The New Diary*. Los Angeles: J. P. Tarcher, 1978.

Promotes diary writing and explains a variety of specific techniques including imagery, lists, altered point of view, unsent letters, maps of consciousness, and dialogues. Wide range of diary applications including dream work and overcoming writing block.

Rico, Gabriele Lusser. *Writing the Natural Way*. Los Angeles: J. P. Tarcher, 1983.

Helps writers find their creative voices through mapping, recurrence, creative tension, and re-vision. Includes brain research and specific strategies that quiet the internal critic.

Routman, Regie. "The Uses and Abuses of Invented Spelling." *Instructor* 102 (9) (May/June 1993): 36–39.

A recognized expert on whole language explains how teachers can get good results from invented spelling.

Tompkins, Gail E. *Teaching Writing: Balancing Process and Product*. Columbus, OH: Merrill, 1990.

Detailed descriptions of teaching various forms of writing across the curriculum for all grade levels. Filled with examples and specific teaching suggestions. One chapter is devoted to journals and other informal writing.

BOOKS TO READ TO CHILDREN

Ahlberg, Janet, and Allen Ahlberg. *The Jolly Postman*. Boston: Little, Brown, 1986.

The jolly postman delivers letters and cards to storybook characters including the Three Bears and Goldilocks. Includes actual missives in built-in envelopes.

Baker, Keith. *The Dove's Letter*. San Diego: Harcourt Brace, 1993.

Beautifully illustrated book about a dove who delivers the same letter to many people in the forest and the village. Each delivery sparks the recipient to rekindle a lost love. Good to use in beginning units on unsent letters for primary students.

Cleary, Beverly. *Dear Mr. Henshaw*. New York: Dell, 1983.

Series of letters written to an author from a sixth-grader's point of view. Insightful, warm, and real. Good examples of unsent letters for intermediate students.

Scieszka, Jon. *The True Story of the Three Little Pigs!* New York: Viking, 1989.

Beautifully illustrated book about the three little pigs and how they framed the poor old wolf. Great for starting altered point of view journals.

Silverstein, Shel. *The Giving Tree*. Harper and Row, 1964.

The relationship between an apple tree and a boy as they age. Good example of altered point of view.